Americana Eb

The Favorite Tipple of our Forefathers and the Laws and Customs Relating Thereto

Hewson L. Peeke

Alpha Editions

This edition published in 2024

ISBN : 9789366384528

Design and Setting By
Alpha Editions
www.alphaedis.com
Email - info@alphaedis.com

As per information held with us this book is in Public Domain. This book is a reproduction of an important historical work. Alpha Editions uses the best technology to reproduce historical work in the same manner it was first published to preserve its original nature. Any marks or number seen are left intentionally to preserve its true form.

Contents

CHAPTER I *Customs Based on Race Source of Population* ......- 1 -
CHAPTER II *Early Attempts at Regulation by Legislation* ....- 6 -
CHAPTER III *Schools and Colleges* ....- 12 -
CHAPTER IV *Bench and Bar* ....- 16 -
CHAPTER V *Church and Clergy* ....- 20 -
CHAPTER VI *Relation of George Washington to the Liquor Traffic* ....- 25 -
CHAPTER VII *The Slave Trade* ....- 36 -
CHAPTER VIII *Christenings—Marriages—Funerals* ....- 50 -
CHAPTER IX *Vendues—Chopping Bees—House Bees—Wood Spells—Clearing Bees* ....- 55 -
CHAPTER X *Extent and Effect of the Traffic at Flood Tide* ...- 63 -

CHAPTER I
Customs Based on Race Source of Population

In order to understand the laws, social habits, and customs in regard to the use of liquor it seems proper to consider briefly the sources of the population of the different states and of the country generally. At the time when America was settled, no European people drank water as we do today for a constant beverage. The English drank ale, the Dutch beer, the French and Spanish light wines, for every day use. Hence it seemed to the colonists a dangerous experiment to drink water in the New World. The Dutch were great beer drinkers and quickly established breweries at Albany and New York. Before the century ended New Englanders had abandoned the constant drinking of ale and beer for cider. Cider was very cheap; but a few shillings a barrel. It was supplied in large amounts to students at college and even very little children drank it. President John Adams was an early and earnest wisher for temperance reform; but, to the end of his life, he drank a large tankard of hard cider every morning when he first got up. It was free in every farmhouse to all travelers and tramps. As years passed on and great wealth came to individuals the tables of the opulent Dutch rivalled the luxury of English and French houses of wealth. When Doctor Cutler dined with Colonel Duer in New York in 1787 there were fifteen kinds of wine served, besides beer, cider, and porter. In the Dutch cellar might be found apples, parsnips, turnips, etc., along with barrels of vinegar, cider, and ale, and canty brown jugs of rum. In the houses of the wealthier classes there was also plenty of wine, either of the claret family or some kind of sack, which was a name covering sherries, canaries, and madeiras. Teetotalism would have been quite unintelligible to the farmer or burgher of those healthy days of breezy activity out of doors. In the Dutch cupboard or on the sideboard always stood the gleaming decanter of cut-glass or the square high-shouldered magnum of aromatic schnapps. The drinking habits of the Dutch colonists were excessive. Tempered in their tastes somewhat by the universal brewing and drinking of beer, they did not use as much as the Puritans of New England, nor drink as deeply as the Virginia planters, but the use of liquor was universal. A libation was poured on every transaction at every happening of the community; in public as well as private life John Barleycorn was a witness at the drawing of a contract, the signing of a deed, the selling of a farm, the purchase of goods, the arbitration of a suit. If a party backed out from a contract he did not back out from the treat. Liquor was served at vendues and made the bidders expansive. It appeared at weddings, funerals, church openings, deacon ordainings, and house raisings. No farm hand in haying, no sailor on a vessel, no workman in a mill, no cobbler, tailor, carpenter, mason, or tinker would work without some strong drink or treat. The bill for liquor where many workmen were employed at a house raising was often a heavy one.

As to New England, Eugene Lawrence in his papers on colonial progress, says, "wines and liquors were freely consumed by our ancestors and even New England had as yet (1775) no high repute for temperance. Rum was taken as a common restorative." The Puritans had no objection to wine, and in latter colonial times hard drinking was very common even among ministers; but they were much opposed to health drinking which was too jovial and pleasant to suit their gloomy principles. Doctor Peters thus speaks of Connecticut:

"The various fruits are in greater perfection than in England. The peach and apple are more luscious, beautiful, and large; one thousand peaches are produced from one tree; five or six barrels of cider from one apple tree. Cider is the common drink at the table. The inhabitants have a method of purifying cider by frost and separating the watery part from the spirit, which, being secured in proper vessels and colored by Indian corn, becomes, in three months so much like Madeira wine, that Europeans drink it without perceiving the difference. They make peachy and perry, grape and currant wines, and good beers of pumpkin, molasses, bran of wheat, spruce, and malt."

Perry was made from pears, as cider is from apples, and peachy from peaches. Metheglin and mead, drinks of the old Druids in England, were made from honey, yeast, and water. In Virginia whole plantations of the honey locust furnished locust beans for making metheglin. From persimmons, elderberries, juniper berries, pumpkins, cornstalks, hickory nuts, sassafras bark, birch bark, and many other leaves and roots various light wines were made. An old song boasted:

Oh we can make liquor to sweeten our lips
Of pumpkins, of parsnips, of walnut-tree chips.

Beer was brewed in families, and the orchards soon yielded an abundance of cider. In 1721 the production of cider increased so that one village of forty families made three thousand barrels, and in 1728 Judge Joseph Wilder, of Lancaster, made six hundred and sixteen barrels himself.

When the Quakers framed their constitution for Pennsylvania they inserted clauses punishing swearing, intemperance, cardplaying, and the drinking of healths. They were mighty drinkers in their sober fashion, consuming vast quantities of ale and spirits, and making no serious inroads on the pure and wholesome water, although we are gravely assured that particular pumps, one on Walnut Street, and one in Norris Alley, were held in especial favor as having the best water in town for the legitimate purpose of boiling greens. Their first beer was made from molasses, and we have Penn's assurance that, when "well boyled with Sassafras or Pine infused into it," this was a very tolerable drink. Rum punch was also in liberal demand, and after a few years the thirsty colonists began to brew ale, and drank it out of deep pewter mugs.

When Congress met in 1774, in Philadelphia, John Adams was shocked by the display of eatables. His appetite overcame his scruples, although after each feast he scourged himself for yielding. After dining with Mr. Miers, a young Quaker lawyer, Adams remarks in his diary:

"A mighty feast again; nothing less than the very best of Claret, Madeira, and Burgundy. I drank Madeira at a great rate and found no inconvenience. This plain Friend and his plain though pretty wife, with her Thees and Thous, had provided us the most costly entertainment, ducks, hams, chickens, beef, pig, tarts, creams, custards, jellies, fools, trifles, floating islands, beer, porter, punch, wine, etc."

Again after dining at Mr. Powell's:

"A most sinful feast again: Everything which could delight the eye, or allure the taste, curds, and creams, jellies, sweetmeats of various kinds, twenty sorts of tarts, fools, trifles, floating islands, whipped syllabubs, etc. Parmesan cheese, punch, wine, porter, beer, etc."

The Swedes planted peach and fruit trees of all kinds, had flourishing gardens, and grew rich selling the products when the Quakers arrived. They made wine, beer, or brandy out of sassafras, persimmons, corn, and apparently anything that could be made to ferment and they imported Madeira. Acrelius, their historian, gives a long list of their drinks, and tells us that they always indulged in four meals a day.

In the *True and Sincere Declaration*, issued in December, 1609, by the Governor and Council for Virginia, there was an advertisement for two brewers, who, as soon as they were secured, were to be dispatched to the Colony. Brewers were also included among the tradesmen who were designed by the Company to go over with Sir Thomas Gates. This indicated the importance in the eyes of that corporation of establishing the means in Virginia of manufacturing malt liquors on the spot instead of relying on the importation from England. The notion arose that one of the principal causes of mortality so prevalent among those arriving in the Colony, in the period following the first settlement of the country, was the substitution of water for beer to which the immigrants had been accustomed in England. The Assembly, in the session of 1623, went so far as to recommend that all new comers should bring in a supply of malt to be used in brewing liquor, thus making it unnecessary to drink the water of Virginia until the body had become hardened to the climate. Previous to 1625, two brew-houses were in operation in the Colony, and the patronage they received was evidently very liberal.

Cider was in as common use as beer; in season it was found in the house of every planter in the Colony. It was the form of consideration in which rent was occasionally settled; the instance of Alexander Moore, of New York, shows the quantity often bequeathed: he left at his decease twenty gallons of raw cider and one hundred and thirty of boiled. Richard Moore of the same county kept on hand as many as fourteen cider casks. Richard Bennett made about twenty butts of cider annually, while Richard Kinsman compressed from the pears growing in his orchard forty or fifty of perry. A supply of spirits was provided for the members of public bodies when they convened. The character of the liquors used depended on the nature of the assemblage. When Charles Hansford and David Condon, as executors of the widow of the unfortunate Thomas Hansford, leased her residence in York to the justice of the peace of that county to serve as a court house, they bound themselves to furnish not only accommodations for horses, but also a gallon of brandy during each session of the bench.

It is not stated whether this brandy was consumed by the honorable justices in the form of the drink which had become so famous in later times in Virginia, the mint julep, but if mint was cultivated in the colony at that age, it is quite probable that a large part of this gallon was converted into that mixture. In 1666 the justices of Lower Norfolk county rented the tract of land on which the court house was situated, on condition that the lessee, in part consideration for the use of the houses and orchards each year, would pay ten gallons brewed from English grain. The members of the Council appear to have been fastidious in their tastes. It was one of the duties of the auditor-general to have a large quantity of wine always ready at hand for this body. Thus on one occasion William Byrd, who filled the office in the latter part of the century, ordered for their use twenty dozen of claret, and six dozen of canary, sherry, and Rhenish, respectively. A quarter of a cask of brandy was also to be added.

CHAPTER II
Early Attempts at Regulation by Legislation

This unrestrained indulgence in liquor, which previous to 1624 had excited the criticism of the company, called down on the Colony on several occasions the animadversion of the Royal Governor after he had taken charge of affairs in Virginia. In 1625 Governor Yeardley was instructed to suppress drunkenness by severe punishments, and to dispose of the spirits brought into the Colony in such manner that it would go to the relief and comfort of the whole plantation instead of falling into the hands of those who would abuse it. He received additional orders to return to the importers all liquors shown to be decayed or unwholesome. The injunction to withhold all liquors imported into the Colony from persons who were guilty of excess in the use of them was repeated.

The attempts to prevent drunkenness were not confined to instructions to the Governors, given by the authorities in England. From the first session of the first assembly, no legislative means were left unemployed to accomplish the same object. In 1619 it was provided that the person guilty in this respect should for the first offense be privately reproved by his minister; for the second, publicly; for the third be imprisoned for twelve hours; and if still incorrigible be punished as the Governor directed.

In March, 1623-4, the church-wardens in every parish were ordered to present all persons guilty of drunkenness to the commander of the plantation. In 1631-2 the offender was required to pay five shillings into the hands of the nearest vestry, and this fine could be made good by levy on his property. In 1657-8 the person guilty of inebriety was punished by a very heavy fine, and also rendered incapable of being a witness in court, or bearing office under the government of the Colony. In 1691 the penalty for drunkenness was ten shillings, and if unable to pay the sum, the offender was to be exposed in the stocks for the space of two hours.

In 1668 there were so many taverns and tippling houses in the Colony that it was found necessary to reduce the number in each county to one or two, unless, for the accommodation of travelers, more should be needed at ports, ferries, and the crossings of great roads, in addition to that which was erected at the court house.

Drunkards were severely punished and were set in the stocks and whipped. On September 3, 1633, in Boston one Robert Coles was "fined ten shillings and enjoined to stand with a white sheet of paper on his back, whereon *Drunkard* shall be written in great lynes, and to stand therewith soe long as the court find meet, for abusing himself shamefully with drinke." Robert Coles for "drunkenness by him committed at Rocksbury shall be disfranchised, weare about his neck, and so to hang upon his outward garment a D made of redd cloth & sett upon white; to continue this for a yeare, & not to have it off any time hee comes among company, under the penalty of one shilling for the first offense, and five pounds for the second, and afterwards to be punished by the Court as they think meet: *also he is to weare the D outwards.*"

Lists of names of common drunkards were given to landlords in some towns, and landlords were warned not to sell liquor to them. Licenses were removed and fines imposed on those who did not heed the warning. The tithing man, that most bumptious public functionary of colonial times, was at first the official appointed to spy specially on the ordinaries. He inspected these houses, made complaints of any disorders he discovered, and gave into the constable the names of idle drinkers and gamers. He warned the keepers of public houses to sell no more liquor to any whom he fancied had been tippling too freely.

John Josslyn, an English visitor in Boston in 1663, complained bitterly thus:

"At houses of entertainment into which a stranger went, he was presently followed by one appointed to that office, who would thrust himself into the company uninvited, and if he called for more drink than the officer thought in his judgment he could soberly bear away, he would presently countermand it, and appoint the proportion, beyond which he could not get one drop."

The prisons found little occupation as compared with the pillory and the whipping post. The latter was the common corrector of drunkenness. We have an amusing description of what constitutes drunkenness, from Colonel Dodberry: "Now for to know a drunken man the better, the Scriptures describes them to stagger and reel to and fro; and so when the same legs which carry a man into the house can not bring him out again, it is a sufficient sign of drunkenness."

In 1676, during the supremacy of Nathaniel Bacon, at which time so many laws were passed for the purpose of suppressing long standing abuses, a legislative attempt was made to enforce what practically amounted to general prohibition. The licenses of all inns, alehouses, and tippling houses, except those at James City, and at the two great ferries of York River, were revoked. The keepers of the ordinaries which were permitted to remain open at the latter places were allowed to sell only beer and cider. This regulation was remarkable in that it was adopted by the action of the people, who must have been the principal customers of the tippling houses, if not of the inns. Not content with putting a stop to sales in public places, the framers of the regulation further prescribed that "no one should presume to sell any sort of drink whatsoever, by retail, under any color, pretence, delusion, or subtle evasion whatsoever, to be drunk or spent in his or their house or houses, upon his or their plantation or plantations."

The general court of Massachusetts on one occasion required the proper officers to notice the apparel of the people, especially their "ribbands and great boots." Drinking of healths in public or private; funeral badges; celebrating the church festivals of Christmas and Easter; and many other things that seemed quite improper to magistrates and legislators, and especially to the Puritan clergy, were forbidden.

In Pennsylvania men were imprisoned in a cage seven feet high, seven feet wide, and seven feet long, for selling liquor to the Indians and for watering the white man's rum, both of which offences the law placed on equal footing.

Virginia and New Jersey declared liquor debts uncollectible by law.

Several of the colonies forbade workmen to be paid in liquor. In Massachusetts, in 1764, the law required that all who bought liquor should render an account of it except state officers, professors and students of Harvard College, and preachers of the gospel.

The law frequently manifested great concern about the clergy. Virginia had a statute making it an offence for a minister to appear drunk in his pulpit on Sunday, and in addition the following statute:

"Ministers shall not give themselves to excess in drinking or riot, spending their time idly by day or by night, playing at dice, cards, or any unlawful game, but at all times convenient they shall hear or read some what of the Holy Scriptures."

It is one of the curiosities of old time legislation that the use of tobacco was in earliest colonial days plainly regarded by the magistrates and elders as far more sinful, degrading, and harmful than indulgence in intoxicating liquors. No one could take tobacco "publicquely" nor in his own house, or anywhere else before strangers. Two men were forbidden to smoke together. No one could smoke within two miles of the meeting house on the Sabbath day. There were wicked backsliders who were caught smoking around the corner of the meeting house, and others in the street, and they were fined and set in the stocks and in cages.

Tariffs

After the thirteen colonies had formed "a more perfect union" the question of revenue caused a heated discussion. Of the many ways through which a sure revenue might flow into the treasury none seemed as desirable as an impost. Of molasses, two millions of gallons came into the country each year. A few hundreds of thousands of these were consumed as food. The remainder were hurried to the Massachusetts distilleries and there made into the far-famed New England rum, which by the fishermen at the Grand Banks was thought much finer than the best that came from Jamaica. All other goods brought into any port in the country were to be taxed at five per cent of their value.

A long list of articles was given on which special duties were to be paid. At the head of the list stood Jamaica rum, which on motion was changed to distilled spirits of Jamaica proof. Two duties were suggested, one of fifteen cents on the gallon, which speedily divided the committee. Some thought such rates too high. Some declared they were much too low. And before the discussion had gone far it turned into a debate on the good and ill effects of high duties and low duties. One low tariff member remarked that the first thing to be considered in laying a tax was the likelihood of gathering it, and that as taxes increased this likelihood decreased. "I trust," said he, "it does not need illustration to convince every member of the committee that a high duty is a very strong temptation to smuggling. Just in the proportion which a tax bears to the value of an article is the risk men will run in their attempts to bring in that article in an illegal way. This impairs the revenue, and in time so much comes in through the hands of smugglers that no revenue is yielded at all." Boudinot said "he for one would be glad to see Jamaica rum doing just that very thing." There were three good results that would come of a high rum tariff: The treasury wanted money, and surely there was no article on the lists of taxable goods so likely to furnish a revenue as rum; the importation would be discouraged, and that was beneficial to the morals of the people; the West Indian distilleries would have no inducement to turn their molasses into rum, and as they had no markets for molasses save those of the United States, the home stills would be set actively to work.

These remarks on the moral effects of the tax were violently attacked by two members from the eastward. Fisher Ames quite forgot himself, and reminded the committee, with great vehemence of gesture and speech, that they were not in church or at school, to sit listening to harangues of speculative piety. We are, exclaimed he, to talk of the political interests committed to our care. When we take up the subject of morality then let our system look toward morality, and not confound itself with revenue and the protection of manufactures. If any man supposes that a mere law can turn the taste of a people from ardent spirits to malt liquors, he has a most romantic notion of legislative power. Lawrence, one of the members from New York, took up the attack. He was for low tariff. "If," said he, "the committee is to reason and act as moralists, the arguments of the member from New Jersey are sound. For it must be the wish of every man of sense to discourage the use of articles so ruinous to health and morals as rum. But we are to act as politicians, not as moralists. Rum, not morality, is to be taxed. Money, not sobriety, is the object of the tax."

The justness of this reasoning was lost on the committee, and spirits of Jamaica proof were taxed at fifteen cents a gallon. The duty finally levied on all distilled spirits was due to the influence of Hamilton, whose first tariff bill also imposed a duty on glass, "with the significant reservation," as Blaine states, "in deference to popular habits that black quart bottles should be admitted free."

Internal Revenue Tax

The system of internal taxation by the federal government began on that memorable day in 1791 when Washington signed the bill laying a duty on domestic distilled spirits; a tax which, proving more harsh in its operations than was expected, was amended in 1792, and after being denounced by legislatures and by mass meetings as oppressive, unequal, and unjust, was openly resisted by the people of western Pennsylvania, who rose in armed rebellion in 1794. In that same year taxes were laid on licenses for retailing wine and liquor, and on the manufacture of snuff, tobacco, and refined sugar, on carriages, and on sales at auction.

In 1801 the taxes on carriages, on licenses for retailing liquor, on snuff and refined sugar, on sales at auction, when about to expire, were continued without a time limit; but the next year the republicans were in control, and every kind of internal tax was abolished with exultation.

With this record behind them the two parties met in the extra session of the thirteenth congress and changed places. The federalists became the enemies of taxation; the republicans became its advocates, and before the session ended taxed pleasure carriages, sales at auction, sugar refineries, salt, licenses to sell liquor at retail; laid a stamp tax on all kinds of legal documents, taxed whiskey stills, imposed a direct tax of three million dollars and brought back all the machinery of assessment and collection, and again turned loose in the land the tax gatherer and what they had once called his minions. As some months must necessarily pass before any money could be raised from these sources, another loan of seven million and a half was authorized. From this time until the present liquor has been constantly taxed both by state and nation, and has been relied on to furnish a large part of the public revenue.

CHAPTER III
Schools and Colleges

What the common schools of a century or two ago must have been is indicated by a description of the colleges which will hereafter be given in this chapter. Many of the school-masters were ignorant, and in addition were much addicted to the use of intoxicating liquors. The first of whom we have any trace was Jan Roelandsen, a New York school-master, who is on record as lying drunk for a month at a time, and being incorrigibly lazy. He was the first of many. Winthrop, in his *History of New England*, describes the censuring of Nathaniel Eton, a school-master, for furnishing insufficient board to his scholars, in which proceeding his wife testified that the bread and beer was always free for the boarders to go to. In 1693 a school bill for a couple of boys of the Lloyd family of Long Island contained the following items:

A bottle of wine for his mistress	10 d.
Wormwood and rubab	6 d.

While the boys took the drugs the school-mistress drank the wine.

Henry Clay's education was in a district school taught in a log cabin by an intemperate Englishman, and consisted of the merest rudiments. Peter Cartwright speaks of his school teacher as a Seceder minister who would get drunk at times. Washington Irving's *Ichabod Crane*, and Eggleston's *Hoosier School-master* are at least average pictures of the country school-masters of an early day. The chorus of the school-masters seems to have been:

"Let schoolmasters puzzle their brains
With grammar and nonsense and learning,
Good liquor I stoutly maintain
Gives genius a better discerning."

MacMasters describes early college life in 1784 as follows:

"The students lodged in the dormitories and ate at the commons. The food then partaken of with thankfulness would now be looked upon as prison fare. At breakfast, which was served at sunrise in summer and at day-break in winter, there was doled out to each student a small can of unsettled coffee, a size of biscuit, and a size of butter weighing generally about an ounce. Dinner was the staple meal, and at this each student was regaled with a pound of meat. Two days in the week, Monday and Thursday, the meat was boiled, and, in college language, these were known as boiling days. On the five remaining days, the meat was roasted, and to them the nickname of roasting days were fastened. With the flesh always went potatoes. When boiling days came round, pudding and cabbage, wild peas and dandelions were added. The only delicacy to which no stint was applied was the cider, a beverage then fast supplanting the small beer of the colonial days. This was brought to the mess in pewter cans which were passed from mouth to mouth, and when emptied were again replenished. For supper there was a bowl of milk and a size of bread."

The oldest college in the United States, that of William and Mary, was founded by the King and Queen of that name, who gave it twenty thousand acres of land and a penny a pound duty on tobacco exported from Virginia and Maryland. The assembly also gave it a duty on imported liquors for its support. This was in 1726, and the proceeds of the tax were to be devoted to its running expenses and the establishment of scholarships. Twenty-five years later the same benevolent body enriched the college with the proceeds of the tax on peddlers. Those who are inclined to throw stones at the source of these benefactions should remember that Harvard College has more than once profited by the gains of an authorized lottery, receiving more than eighteen thousand dollars from such a source as late as 1805.

In 1752 the rules of William and Mary College required that "spirituous liquors were to be used in that moderation which became the prudent and industrious student." From the list were excluded all liquids but beer, cider, toddy, and spirits and water. In 1798, when the Bishop of Virginia was president of the college and had apartments in the building, the English traveler Weld noticed that half a dozen or more of the students dined at his table one day when he was there. "Some were without shoes and stockings, others without coats. During the meal they constantly rose to help themselves from the sideboard."

William and Mary College, during the days of Jefferson and Monroe, was "a riot of pleasure and power, a jumble of royalist splendor and patriotic fervor, an awe of learning, and indulgence of *vice*." Thomas Jefferson, the most eminent graduate of the college, and its cordial friend, in advanced life remembered the "regular annual riot and battles between the students and the town boys;" and bore testimony to other greater evils. From one source and another have come down to us complaints that the college was neither a college, nor a grammar school, nor an Indian hospital; that its teachers squabbled among themselves to the detriment of their academic work; and that some of the professors sent out by the bishops of London were drunken, quarrelsome, and ignorant of the subjects they professed to teach.

The president, representing the bishop, might have brought charges against the clergy for their flagrant drunkenness but he refrained, being himself a notorious drunkard. Farquier, representative of the crown, was the most finished gentleman Virginia had known, and also the most demoralizing. He introduced a passion for high play that ruined many a fine old family, encouraged hard drinking and a mania for racing, delighted in having the clergy and favored students join him in his all-night revels.

Commencement at Harvard in Old New England days was a fête indeed; a fête so important as to be attended by giant expenditures and sinful extravagance. Indeed, so early as 1722 in its history, an act was passed "that henceforth no preparation nor provision of either Plumb Cake, or Roasted, Boyled or Baked Meats or Pyes of any kind shall be made by any Commencer," and that "no such have any distilled liquors in his Chamber or any composition therewith," under penalty of twenty shillings or forfeiture of the said provisions. Five years later several acts were passed "for preventing the Excesses, Immoralities and Disorders of the Commencements," by way of enforcing the foregoing act. These, with a simplicity of conclusion which brings a smile, declare that "if any who now doe or hereafter shall stand for their degrees, presume to doe anything contrary to the said Act or goe about to evade it by Plain Cake," they shall forfeit the honors of the college.

In the latter part of the eighteenth century the Yale College butler held his buttery in the ground floor, front corner room, of South Middle College, and sold cider, metheglin, strong beer, together with loaf sugar, etc., to the students. Dr. Lyman

Beecher, in his autobiography, says of old Doctor Dwight, then president of the college: "Before he came college was in a most ungodly state.... Wine and liquor were kept in many rooms, intemperance, profanity, gambling, and licentiousness were common."

John Bacon, afterwards United States Senator, and Chief Justice of New Hampshire, sailed from Boston for Princeton College September 10, 1751. In his diary he states his outfit.

5 qts West India rum	5	17	6
1 qr. lb. Tea,		12	
1 doz. fowls,	2	10	
2 lbs. loaf sugar,		16	
1 doz-8 lemons,	1	9	
3 lbs. butter,		12	

In a book published in 1764 describing student life at Princeton, it is stated that "the general table drink is beer or cider."

Washington Irving, in *Salmagundi*, described seeing two students at the tavern at Princeton who got drunk and cursed the professors. Madison was a *poler* at Princeton, and although the five o'clock horn was a sovereign preventive of midnight revelry, Madison was occasionally found around the blazing logs of the Nassau Inn, when tankards of ale and puffs at the long stemmed pipes punctuated the students' songs.

James Buchanan at Dickinson was the typical *bad boy*. Immorality was rampant among the students, sobriety and books were ridiculed. Buchanan became a leader in debauchery, although his physique enabled him at the same time to maintain a high rank in scholarship. The faculty chose him as a scapegoat, and he was expelled.

Benny Havens, the hero of the West Point song, for many years sold liquor illicitly to the cadets. The foundation of Vassar College was the fortune acquired by Matthew Vassar as a brewer.

CHAPTER IV
Bench and Bar

The field which then lay before the ablest lawyers was far less extensive and far less lucrative than at present. Thousands of cases now arise which could not then have possibly arisen. No wealthy corporations existed, expending each year in lawyers' fees enough money to have paid the taxes of the four colonies of New England. Patent law and railroad law, the business of banks and insurance companies, express companies, telegraph companies, and steamships, have given rise to legal questions of which neither Parsons, nor Tudor, nor Dexter had any conception whatever. A fee of $20,000 was unknown; a suit involving $50,000,000 was unheard of. Yet the profession was not ill-paid and offered many incentives to bright young men. The law student of that day usually began by offering his services to some lawyer of note, and if they were accepted he paid a fee of a hundred dollars, and began to read law books and copy briefs. In the course of two years he was expected to have become familiar with *Coke on Littleton*, with Wood's *Institutes of Civil Law*, with *Piggot on Conveyances*, with Burns's *Justice of the Peace*, with Hawkin's *Pleas of the Crown*, with Salkeld's *Reports*, with Lillie's *Abridgements*, and with some work on chancery practice and some work on what would now be called international law. This accomplished, his patron would take him into court, seat him at the lawyers' table, whisper to the gentlemen present, and with their consent would rise and ask leave of the court to present a young man for the oath of an attorney. The court would ask if the bar consented. The lawyers would then bow. The patron would vouch for the morals and learning of his young friend, and the oath would be administered by the clerk. This done, the new attorney would be introduced to the bar and carried off to the nearest tavern where health and prosperity would be drunk to him in bumpers of strong punch.

Thaddeus Stevens has left an amusing account of his brief connection, about 1820, with the Maryland bar. The examination took place in the evening before the judge and the bar committee. His honor informed Stevens that there was one indispensable requisite to the examination. "There must be two bottles of Madeira on the table and the applicant must order it in." Stevens complied with the condition, and, after the wine had been disposed of, one of the committee asked the applicant what books he had read. He replied, "*Blackstone, Coke upon Littleton*, a work on Pleading, and *Gilbert on Evidence*." He was then asked two or three questions, the last of which related to the difference between executory devises and a contingent remainder. A satisfactory answer to this question led his honor again to intervene. "Gentlemen," said the judge, "you see the young man is all right. I will give him a certificate." But before the certificate was delivered, the candidate was informed that usage required that the ceremony should terminate in the same way it had opened, and that two more bottles must be produced. Stevens very willingly complied with this requirement and was made a member of the bar.

With such a bar the courts were rude and primitive. The courts sat often times in taverns, where the tedium of business was relieved by glasses of grog, while the judge's decisions were not put on record, but were simply shouted by the crier from the inn door at the nearest market place. In North Carolina the laws were not printed for a long time but only read aloud in the market place, and the courts and legislature met in private houses and taverns.

Probably the best type of the judges produced by this system was old Chief Justice Marshall, who occupied the highest seat in the Supreme Court of the United States for 35 years. His decisions were recorded and will be the noblest monument a man could have or wish. In reference to two of them, Judge Story says: "If all the acts of his judicial life or arguments had perished, his luminous judgments on these occasions would give an enviable immortality to his name." Judge Story said of the mode of life of the judges at these general terms of the court:

"Our intercourse is perfectly familiar and unrestrained, and our social hours, when undisturbed with the labors of law, are passed in gay and frank conversation, which at once enlivens and instructs. We take no part in Washington society. We dine once a year with the President, and that is all. On other days we dine together, and discuss at table the questions which are argued before us. We are great ascetics and even deny ourselves wine except in wet weather. What I say about the wine gives you our rule; but it does sometimes happen that the Chief Justice will say to me, when the cloth is removed, 'Brother Story, step to the window and see if it does not look like rain.'

And if I tell him the sun is shining brightly, Justice Marshall will sometimes reply, 'All the better, for our jurisdiction extends over so large a territory that the doctrine of chances makes it certain that it must be raining somewhere.' The Chief was brought up on Federalism and Madeira, and he is not the man to outgrow his early prejudices. The best Madeira was that labelled 'The Supreme Court,' as their Honors, the Justices, used to make a direct importation every year, and sip it as they consulted over the cases before them every day after dinner, when the cloth had been removed."

Returning to lawyers, Henry Clay was extremely convivial, keenly enjoying the society of his friends. He was fastidious in his tastes though far from being an epicure. He indulged moderately in wine, took snuff, and used tobacco freely. In earlier days he lost and won large sums of money at play but ceased the practice of gaming in consequence of censure, though he remained inveterately fond of whist.

Webster was majestic in his consumption of liquor as in everything else. Parton in his Essay speaks of seeing Webster at a public dinner "with a bottle of Madeira under his yellow waistcoat and looking like Jove." Schuyler Colfax frequently spoke of seeing Webster so drunk that he did not know what he was doing. Josiah Quincy describes Webster's grief at the burning of his house because of the loss of half a pipe of Madeira wine. John Sherman in his *Recollections* describes hearing Webster deliver a speech at a public dinner when intoxicated.

"In ante-bellum days, at this season of the year, when there was a long session, a party went down the Potomac every Saturday on the steamboat Salem to eat planked shad. It was chiefly composed of Senators and Representatives, with a few leading officials, some prominent citizens, and three or four newspaper men, who in those days never violated the amenities of social life by printing what they heard there. An important house in Georgetown would send on board the steamer large demijohns filled with the best wines and liquors, which almost everybody drank without stint. Going down the river there was a good deal of card playing in the upper saloon of the boat, with some story telling on the hurricane deck. Arriving at the white house fishing grounds, some would go on shore, some would watch the drawing of the seine from the boat, some would take charge of the culinary department, and a few would remain at the card tables. The oaken planks used were about two inches thick, fourteen inches wide, and two feet long. These were scalded and then wiped dry. A freshly caught shad was then taken, scaled, split open down the back, cleaned, washed and dried. It was then spread out on a plank and nailed to it with iron pump tacks. The plank with the fish on it was then stood at an angle of forty-five degrees before a hot wood fire and baked until it was a rich dark brown color, an attendant turning the plank every few moments and basting the fish with a thin mixture of melted butter and flour. Meanwhile an experienced cook was frying fresh shad roe in a mixture of eggs and cracker dust at another fire. The planked shad, meanwhile, were served on the planks on which they had been cooked, each person having a plank and picking out what portion he liked best, breaking up his roast potato on the warm shad, while the roe was also served to those who wished for it. After the fish came punch and cigars and then they reëmbarked and the bows of the steamer were turned toward Washington. When opposite Alexandria an account was taken of the liquor and wine which had been drunk, and an assessment was levied, which generally amounted to about $2.00 each. I never saw a person intoxicated at one of these shad bakes, nor heard any quarreling."

It is said that Webster went fishing the day before he was to deliver his welcome to Lafayette, and got drunk. As he sat on the bank he suddenly drew from the water a large fish and in his majestic voice said, "Welcome, illustrious stranger, to our shores." The next day his friends, who went fishing with him, were electrified to hear him begin his speech to Lafayette with these same words.

CHAPTER V
Church and Clergy

The first tavern at Cambridge, Massachusetts, was kept by a deacon of the church, afterwards, steward of Harvard college; and the relation of tavern and meeting house did not end with their simultaneous establishment, but they continued the most friendly neighbors. Licenses to keep houses of entertainment were granted with the condition that the tavern must be near the meeting-house—a keen contrast to our present laws prohibiting the sale of liquor within a certain distance of a church. Those who know the oldtime meeting house can fully comprehend the desire of the colonists to have a tavern near at hand, especially during the winter services. Through autumn rains and winter frosts and snows the poorly built meeting house stood unheated, growing more damp, more icy, more deadly, with each succeeding week. Women cowered shivering, half-frozen, over the feeble heat of a metal footstove as the long services dragged on and the few coals became ashes. Men stamped their feet and swung their arms in the vain effort to warm the blood. Gladly and cheerfully did the whole crowd troop from the gloomy meeting house to the cheerful tavern to thaw out before the afternoon service, and to warm up before the ride or walk home in the late afternoon. It was a scandal in many a town that godly church members took too freely of tavern cheer at the nooning; the only wonder is that the entire congregation did not succumb in a body to the potent flip and toddy of the tavern-keeper. In mid-summer the hot sun beat down on the meeting house roof, and the burning rays poured in the unshaded windows. The tap-room of the tavern and the green trees in its dooryard offered a pleasant shade to tired church-goers, and its well sweep afforded a grateful drink to those who turned not to the tap-room. There are ever back-sliders in every church community; many walked into the ordinary door instead of up the church alley. The chimney seat of the inn was more comfortable than the narrow seat of the "pue." The general court of Massachusetts passed a law requiring all inn-keepers within a mile of any meeting house to clear their houses "during the hours of the exercise." "Thus," Mr. Field says wittily, "the townsmen were frozen out of the tavern to be frozen in the meeting house." Our ancestors had no reverence for a church save as a literal meeting house, and it was not unusual to transform the house of God into a tavern. The Great House at Charlestown, Massachusetts, the official residence of Governor Winthrop, became a meeting house in 1633, and then a tavern, the Three Cranes, kept by Robert Leary and his descendants for many years. It was destroyed in June, 1775, in the burning of the town.

The first revenue relinquished by the West India Company to the town of New Amsterdam was the excise on wine, beer, and spirits, and the sole condition made by Stuyvesant on its surrender was as to its application, that the salaries of the Dominies should be paid from it. For a year beginning November, 1661, the burghers of Esopus paid a tax on liquor, the proceeds of which were used to build a parsonage for the minister. St. Philip's church in Charleston, South Carolina, was originally built by a tax of two pence a gallon on spirits imported in 1670. Between 1743 and 1750 the public revenues of South Carolina were all raised by three per cent duties on liquors, wines, sugar, molasses, slaves, and imported dry-goods, and produced about forty-five hundred pounds, of which one thousand pounds were devoted to paying the salaries of ten ministers. The dedication of St. Michael's church in Charleston, South Carolina, was followed by a great dinner, at which a large amount of liquor was consumed.

Under such circumstances it could not be expected that the clergy would be much troubled with scruples on the use of liquor, and the evidence is that they were not. We must bear in mind that the use of liquors was universal in those days. "Ordination Day" was almost as great a day for the tavern as for the meeting house. The visiting ministers who came to assist at the religious service of ordination of a new minister were usually entertained at the tavern. Often a specially good beer was brewed called "ordination beer," and in Connecticut an "ordination ball" was given at the tavern—this with the sanction of the parsons. The bills for entertaining the visitors for the dinner and lodging at the local taverns are in many cases preserved. One of the most characteristic was at a Hartford ordination. It runs:

	To keeping ministers,	£	s.	d.
2	mugs toddy,		2	4
5	Segars,		5	10
1	pint wine,		3	9

3	Lodgings,		9	
3	Bitters,			9
3	Breakfasts,		3	6
15	Boles punch,	1	10	
24	Dinners,	1	16	
11	bottles wine,		3	6
5	Mugs flip,		5	10
5	Boles Punch,		6	
3	Boles Toddy,		3	6

The bill is endorsed with unconscious humor, "This is all paid for except the Minister's Rum."

Here is another ordination bill:

30	Boles of Punch before the People went to meeting.
10	bottles of wine before they went to meeting.
44	Bowles of Punch while at dinner.
18	bottles of wine.
8	Bowles of Brandy.
	Cherry rum [quantity not mentioned].

When the fathers met in synod at Cambridge in 1648, there was a liquor bill in connection with the expense of the meeting. At the ordination of Edwin Jackson in Woburn, 1729, the town paid for six and one-half barrels of cider, 25 gallons of wine, 2 gallons of brandy, 4 gallons of rum.

In the South the clergy were addicted to horse racing, gambling, and drunken revels. One of them was for many years president of a Jockey Club. They encouraged among the people the celebration of the sacrament of baptism with music and dancing in which the clergymen took part, a custom which shows signs of returning in England. One fought a duel in a churchyard, another thrashed his vestry. One parson preached in his stocking feet, one in his study coat, and one ran a distillery. Many of them were appointed by the British government and by the Bishop of London and they were affected by the irreligious listlessness and low moral tone of the English church in the eighteenth century.

Alexander Graydon tells us that in his early days any jockeying, fiddling, wine-bibbing clergyman not over-scrupulous about stealing sermons was currently known as "a Maryland Parson." The Maryland clergy are said to have been more vicious than those of Virginia. They raced horses, hunted foxes, drank, gambled, joined in every amusement of the planters and would extort marriage fees from the poor by breaking off in the middle of the service and refusing to go on until paid.

One Dr. Beatty was acting as chaplain to an army of five hundred men led by Franklin to defend the frontier against the French and Indians after the burning of the Moravian mission at Gnadenhutten, Pennsylvania. "Dr. Beatty complained to me," says Franklin, "that the men did not generally attend his prayers and exhortations. When they were enlisted, they were promised, besides hay and provisions, a gill of rum a day, which was punctually served out to them, half in the morning, and the other half in the evening; and I observed they were as punctual in attending to receiving it; upon which I said to Mr. Beatty, 'It is perhaps below the dignity of your profession to act as steward of the rum, but if you were to deal it out, and only just after prayers you would have them all about you.'" The shrewd suggestion was adopted by Dr. Beatty, and the philosophic Franklin says "Never were prayers more generally and punctually attended; so that I thought this method preferable to the punishment inflicted by some military laws for non-attendance at divine service."

This chapter may well be concluded with the famous and oft quoted letter of Cotton Mather to John Higginson:

> "September ye 15, 1682.

"To ye Aged and Beloved Mr. John Higginson:

"There is now at sea a ship called the Welcome, which has on board an hundred or more of the heretics and malignants called Quakers, with W. Penn, who is the chief scamp, at the head of them.

"The general court has accordingly given secret orders to Master Malachi Huscott, of the brig Porpoise, to waylay the said Welcome, slyly, as near the Cape of Cod as may be, and make captive the said Penn and his ungodly crew, so that the

Lord may be glorified, and not mocked on the soil of this new country with the heathen worship of these people. Much spoil can be made by selling the whole lot to Barbadoes, where slaves fetch good prices in rum and sugar, and we shall not only do the Lord great service by punishing the wicked, but we shall make great good for his minister and people.

"Master Huscott feels hopeful, and I will set down the news when the ship comes back.

"Yours in ye bowels of Christ,
"COTTON MATHER."

CHAPTER VI
Relation of George Washington to the Liquor Traffic

In approaching the study of the character of Washington a writer should always remember the veneration in which his memory is justly held among Americans. The reader should remember that public sentiment was then at a very low ebb with regard to the liquor traffic and neither the drinker nor seller was discredited by his neighbors as he is today.

The use of liquor played an important part in the life of a Virginia planter a century and a half ago. At all the cross-roads and court-houses there sprang up taverns or ordinaries, and in these the men of a neighborhood would gather and over a bowl of punch or a bottle of wine, the expense of which they clubbed to share, would spend their evenings. Into this life Washington eagerly entered. As a mere lad his ledger records expenditures:

"By a club in Arrack at Mr. Gordon's 2/6;

Club of a bottle of Rhenish at Mitchel's 1/3;

To part of the club at Port Royal 1/;

To cash in part for a bowl of fruit punch 1/7-1/2."

When Governor Dinwiddie sent Washington in 1753 with a letter to M. de St. Pierre, the French commander, to remonstrate against the erection of French forts, one of the incidents of his journey was a complimentary visit to the Indian queen, Aliquippa, who resided at the confluence of the Monongahela and Youghiogany rivers, in the southeastern part of Alleghany county, Pennsylvania. She had complained of his neglect in not calling upon her when on his outward journey. Young Washington explained the circumstances that prevented him, and with an apology he gave her a coat and a bottle of rum. The latter, Washington wrote, "was thought the much better present of the two," and harmony of feeling was restored. Aliquippa, who was a woman of great energy and had performed some brave deeds, was held in deep respect, amounting almost to reverence, by the Indians in western Pennsylvania.

In 1766 Washington shipped an unruly negro to the West Indies and wrote the captain of the vessel as follows:

"With this letter comes a negro (Tom) which I beg the favor of you to sell in any of the islands you may go to, for whatever he will fetch, and bring me in return for him

One hhd of best molasses

One ditto of best rum

One barrel of lymes, if good and cheap

One pot of tamarinds, containing about 10 lbs.

Two small ditto of mixed sweetmeats, about 5 lbs each.

And the residue, much or little in good old spirits."

Shortly before this time Washington was a candidate for the legislature. There was then a Virginia statute forbidding treating the voters, or bribery at elections, and declaring illegal all elections thus obtained, yet the following is the bill of the liquors Washington furnished the voters of Frederick:

40 gallons of Rum punch a 3/6 per galn.	7.00
15 gallons of wine a 10 per galn.	7.10
Dinner for your friends	3.00
13 1/2 gallons of wine a 10/	6.15
13 gallons of beer a 1/3	4-4/2
8 qts Cider Royal a 1/6	.16-3
Punch	3-9
30 galls strong beer a 8d. per gall.	1-0
26 gall. best Barbadoes rum 5/	6.10
12 lbs. S Fefd. Sugar 1/6	.18-9
3 galls & 3 qts of beer 1/per gall.	3-9
10 bowls of punch 2/6 each	1.50
9 half pints of rum 7½ d. each	5-7-1
1 pint of wine	1-6

After the election was over, Washington wrote Wood that "I hope no exception was taken to any that voted against me, but that all were alike treated, and all had enough. My only fear is that you spent with too sparing a hand." It is hardly necessary to say that such methods reversed the former election: Washington secured three hundred and ten votes, and Swearington received forty-five. From this time until he took command of the army Washington was a burgess. Once again he was elected from Frederick county, and then, in 1765, he stood for Fairfax, in which Mount Vernon was located. Here he received 208 votes, his colleague getting 148, and in the election of 1768 he received 185, and his colleague only 142. Washington spent between £40 and £75 at each of these elections, and usually gave a ball to the voters on the night he was chosen. Some of the miscellaneous election expenses noted in his ledger are:

54 galls of strong beer

52 dro. of Ale

£1.0.0. to Mr. John Muir for his fiddler,

For cakes at the election £7.11.1.

Bushrod Washington, made a real estate investment that did not suit his uncle, and Washington wrote him as follows:

"Now let me ask you what your views were in purchasing a Lott in a place which, I presume, originated with and will end in two or three Gin shops, which probably will exist no longer than they serve to ruin the proprietors, and those who make the most frequent applications to them."

He expressed an adverse opinion of the liquor business at one time, somewhat in the same line, in a contract he made with a plantation overseer:

"And whereas, there are a number of whiskey stills very contiguous to the said Plantations, and many idle, drunken and dissolute people continually resorting to the same, priding themselves in debauching sober and well-inclined persons, the said Edd Violet doth promise as well for his own sake as his employers to avoid them as he ought."

To the contrary, in hiring a gardener it was agreed as part of the compensation that the man should have "four dollars at Christmas with which he may be drunk for four days and nights; two dollars at Easter to effect the same purpose; two dollars at Whitsuntide to be drunk for two days; a dram in the morning, and a drink of grog at dinner at noon."

At Valley Forge he complained to Congress of the mortifications they (even the general officers) must suffer, when they cannot invite a French officer, a visiting friend, or a traveling acquaintance, to a better repast than stinking whiskey (and not always that) and a bit of beef without vegetables.

In the New York State Library at Albany is a statement in Washington's handwriting of his household expenses for three months at the beginning of his first term as President, from May 24 to August 24, 1789; the total expense for that time was £741 and 9 shillings, of which the following items were for liquor:

	Pounds	Shillings	Pence
Madeira	43	18	
Claret	21	11	
Champaign	18		
Van de Graves			
Cherry	2	5	
Arack	2	16	
Spirits	12		
Brandy	6	6	
Cordials	5	6	
Porter	16	8	
Beer	34	14	6
Cider	4	10	

In the same library is a memorandum of Washington's opinion of his general officers, prepared in the winter of 1791-2. From this it seems that he considered the drinking habit of his subordinates, even at that time, in appointing a successor to General Arthur St. Clair, who had just then been defeated by the Indians:

"Majr General (By Brevet) Wayne.

"More active and enterprising than judicious no economist it is feared—open to flattery—vain—easily imposed upon and liable to be drawn into scrapes. Too indulgent [the effect perhaps of some of the causes just mentioned] to his officers and men. Whether sober—or a little addicted to the bottle, I know not.

"Majr General (By Brevet) Weedon.

"Not supposed to be an officer of much resource, though not deficient of a competent share of understanding—rather addicted to ease and pleasure, and no enemy it is said to the bottle—never has had his name brot forward on this account.

"Major General (By Brevet) Hand.

"A sensible and judicious man, his integrity unimpeached, and was esteemed a pretty good officer. But if I recollect rightly not a very active one. He has never been charged with intemperance to my knowledge. His name has rarely been mentioned under the present difficulty of choosing an officer to command, but this may, in a great measure be owing to his being at a distance.

"Majr General (By Brevet) Scott.

"Brave and means well; but is an officer of inadequate abilities for extreme command, and by report is addicted to drinking."

In 1795, when the United States passed an excise law, distilling became particularly profitable, and a still was set up on his plantation. In this whiskey was made from "rye" chiefly, and Indian corn in a certain proportion, and this not merely used much of the estate's product of those two grains, but quantities were purchased from elsewhere. In 1798 the profit from the distillery was three hundred and forty-four pounds, twelve shillings, and seven and three-quarter pence, with a stock carried over of seven hundred and fifty-five and one-quarter gallons; but this was the most successful year. Cider, too, was made in large quantities.

Washington resigned his command December 23, 1783, and went back to his estate, which had suffered from his eight years' absence. To his friends he offered unpretentious hospitality. "My manner of living is plain," he said, "a glass of wine and a bit of mutton are always ready and such as will be content to partake of them are always welcome."

At Washington's official dinners ordinarily a boiled leg of mutton was served, followed by a glass of wine. The silver service was massive, being valued at $30,000, but the menu was very simple. On a great occasion it included soup, fish roasted and boiled, meats, fowls, and so on, and for dessert, apple pies, puddings, ice cream, jelly, and fruit. After the cloth had been removed the President filled his glass and drank the health by name of each one present.

Samuel Stearns, who was a frequent visitor to Mount Vernon, thus described the habits of Washington:

"He is very regular, temperate and industrious; rises in winter and summer at the dawn of day; generally reads or writes some time before breakfast; breakfasts about seven o'clock on three small Indian hoe cakes, and as many dishes of tea, and often rides immediately to his different farms, and remains with his laborers until a little after two o'clock, then returns and dresses. At three he dines, commonly on a single dish, and drinks from half a pint to a pint of Madeira wine. This with one small glass of punch, a draught of beer, and two dishes of tea (which he takes half an hour before the setting of the sun) constitutes his whole sustenance until the next day. But his table is always furnished with elegance and exuberance; and whether he has company or not, he remains at the table an hour in familiar conversation, then every one is called upon to give some absent friend a toast. After he has dined, he applies himself to business, and about nine retires to rest; but when he has company he attends politely upon them till they wish to withdraw."

Relation of Other Prominent Americans to the Liquor Traffic

Among the early prominent American characters the total abstainer was a rare article, and the prohibitionist almost unknown. Governor John Winthrop was probably a total abstainer, and the romantic character of John Smith seems quite clear from the drinking habits of the period. "Never was warrior known," says an old writer, "from debts and dice and oaths so free," and his own words as to the object of life show a loftiness of purpose almost unknown among his contemporaries, and should be preserved for the example they furnish to posterity. "Seeing we are not born for ourselves but each to help the other, and our abilities are much alike at the hour of our birth and the minute of our death; seeing our good deeds and our bad by faith in Christ's merits is all we have to carry our souls to heaven or hell; seeing honor is our lives' ambition and our ambition after death to have an honorable memory of our life; and seeing by no means we would be abated of the dignities and glories of our predecessors let us imitate their virtues so as to be worthily their successors." So wrote the man of whom old Thomas Fuller said, "He had a prince's heart in a beggar's purse," and to whom one of his comrades, a survivor of the starving time, paid this touching tribute: "Thus we lost him that in all our proceedings made justice his first guide—ever hating baseness, sloth, pride and indignity more than any dangers; that never allowed himself more than his soldiers with him; that upon no occasion would he send them where he would not go himself; that would never see us want what he either had or could by any means get us; that would rather want than borrow or starve than not pay; that loved actions more than words and hated falsehood and covetousness worse than death; whose adventures were our lives and whose loss our deaths."

But these are two of the few oases in the dreary desert of early American drunkenness. Most prominent men of the time drank to excess. The early colonial grandees furnish a number of quaint pictures. Governor William Cosby, of New York, was admitted to the Humdrum Club on January 24, 1733, over many bowls of punch made from peculiar and valuable receipts, known only to the members of the club, which was potent in its effects even over a well seasoned veteran like the late Governor of Minorca. Sir Danvers Osborne, another governor, committed suicide. The colony of New York had been treated to a variety of rulers since the English had taken possession of the Dutch colony. They were endowed with every vice known. They were fortunately spared the dominion of a madman who succeeded a dipsomaniac in the chief office of the province. Governor Clinton immured himself in the fort and spent his time with his bottle and a little trifling circle who lived on his bounty. Governor Hunter was a man of violent passion. After he had had one of his fits an Indian said to an officer, "The governor is drunk." "No," said the officer, "he never drinks any strong liquor." The brave replied, "I do not mean he is drunk with rum, he was born drunk."

In 1688, in the midst of the rejoicings, the news came that the Queen, the second wife of James, had been blessed with a son, who became heir to the throne. The event was celebrated the same evening by bonfires in the streets and a feast at the city hall. At the latter, Mayor Van Courtlandt became so hilarious, that he made a burnt sacrifice to his loyalty of his hat and periwig, waving the burning victims over the banquet table on the point of his straight sword. And when, in March, 1691, Governor Sloughter arrived, and Leisler sent him a letter loyally tendering to him the fort and province, that functionary, under the influence of the aristocratic leaders, answered it by sending an officer to arrest the "usurper" and Milborne and six of the "inferior insurgents" on a charge of high treason. They were taken to prison, and when they were arraigned, the two principal offenders, denying the authority of the court, refused to plead, and appealed to the King. They were condemned and sentenced to death, but Sloughter, who in his sober moments was just and honest, refused to sign the death warrant until he should hear from the King. The implacable enemies of the "usurper," determined on causing his destruction, invited the governor to a dinner party on Staten Island on a bright day in May. One of them carried to the banquet a legally drawn death warrant, and when the governor had been made stupid with liquor, he was induced to sign the fatal paper. It was sent to the city that evening, and on the following morning Leisler and Milborne were summoned to prepare for execution. Leisler sent for his wife, Alice, and their older children, and after a sorrowful parting with them, he and his son-in-law were led to the gallows in a drenching rain. They confessed their errors of judgment but denied all intentional wrongdoing. The blamelessness of their lives confirmed their declarations of innocence. Before Sloughter was permitted to recover from his debauch, they were hanged. It was foul murder. The governor was tortured with remorse for his act, and died of delirium tremens three months afterward.

When William Penn, in 1682, drew up his code of laws for Pennsylvania he made the drinking of healths and the selling of liquor to Indians crimes. His opinion as to drinking healths must have changed between 1682 and 1710 when Dean Swift met Penn and passed a lively evening. He writes Stella, "We sat two hours drinking as good wine as you do," and it is the strongest proof of Penn's lovableness that after drinking good wine with him for two hours that night, Swift the next morning has no word of dispraise for his companion.

One of the oddest characters in early Virginia history was Dr. John Pott, who was at one time governor of Virginia, and is described as a Master of Arts, well practiced in chirurgery and physic and expert also in distilling waters, besides many other ingenious devices. It seems he was also very fond of tasting distilled waters, and at times was more of a boon companion than quite comported with his dignity, especially after he had come to be governor. A letter of George Sandys says of Dr. Pott: "At first he kept too much company with his inferiors who hung upon him while his good liquor lasted." After Harvey's arrival Ex-Governor Pott was held to answer two charges. One was for having abused the power entrusted to him by pardoning a culprit who had been convicted of wilful murder, the other was for stealing cattle. The first charge was a common notoriety; on the second Doctor Pott was tried by a jury and found guilty. The ex-governor was not a pardoner of felony but was a felon himself. The affair reads like a scene in comic opera. Some reluctance was felt about inflicting vulgar punishment upon an educated man of good social position, so he was not sent to jail but confined in his own house, while Sir John Harvey wrote to the King for instructions in the matter. He informed the King that Doctor Pott was by far the best physician in the colony and indeed the only one skilled in epidemics and recommended that he should be pardoned. Accordingly the doctor was set free and forthwith resumed his practice.

No one was better disposed toward a moderate conviviality than Franklin himself. In that old house on High street where he lived and died there remains now in the possession of the Pennsylvania Historical Society that delightful punch-keg which rolled so easily from guest to guest, and which carried the generous liquor generously around Franklin's board. A curious little keg this, pretty, portly, and altogether unlike other punch-bowls left us from colonial days. Among the china was a fine large jug for beer, to stand in the cooler. Franklin's wife was frugal, and it pleased him to set aside her customary frugality on the blithesome occasions when the punch-keg went rolling round.

In 1768, when the advent of the new governor made necessary the election of a new House of Burgesses, Jefferson already craved the opportunity to take an active part in affairs, and at once offered himself as a candidate for Albemarle county. He kept open house, distributed limitless punch, stood by the polls politely bowing to every voter who named him according to the Virginia fashion of the day, and had the good fortune, by these meritorious efforts, to win success. In 1794 Jefferson very nearly sympathized with the Whiskey Rebellion. He called the excise law an infernal one. In his gloomy views of the War of 1812 he asks what Virginia can raise, and answers his question thus: "Tobacco? It is not worth the pipe it is smoked in. Some say whiskey, but all mankind must become drunkards to consume it." While Chastellux, in his travels, tells of discussing a bowl of punch with Jefferson at Monticello, Jefferson never seems to have drunk ardent spirits or strong wine, and in his last illness his physician could not induce him to take brandy strong enough to benefit him.

While Hamilton favored the whiskey tax and caused the Whiskey Rebellion thereby, he nevertheless was in favor of temperance, as is shown by the circulars he issued to the army.

In his early youth Andrew Jackson was gay, careless, rollicking, fond of drinking, horse-racing, cock-fighting, and all kinds of mischief; his habits moderated in later years and in his old age Jackson became religious.

The son of Dolly Madison by her first marriage, Payne Todd, was a continual financial burden to her even after the death of President Madison, and by his dissipation broke his mother's heart, embittered her old age, and ruined her financially as if to show that even the wife of the President was not exempt from the burdens of any mother of a drunkard. When Tyler became President he lived precisely as he had done on his Virginia plantation. He invariably invited visitors to visit the family dining-room, and "take something," from a sideboard well garnished with decanters of ardent spirits and wine, with a bowl of juleps in the summer, and of eggnog in the winter.

One of the most picturesque figures of this period was General Sam Houston, who was a prominent figure at Washington during the Taylor administration. Because of trouble with his wife he resigned the governorship of Tennessee, went into the Cherokee country, adopted the Indian costume and became an Indian trader and so dissipated that his Indian name was "Big-drunk." He wore a waistcoat made from the skin of a panther dressed with the hair on, and was conspicuous in the Senate for whittling soft pine sticks, which were provided him by the seargeant-at-arms. He was the best customer supplied from his own whiskey barrel, until one day after a prolonged debauch he heard that the Mexicans had taken up arms against their revolted province. He cast off his Indian attire, dressed like a white man, and never touched a drop of any intoxicating beverage afterwards.

CHAPTER VII
The Slave Trade

In no branch of history is the culpability of the liquor traffic more thoroughly shown than in its relation to the slave trade. The making of rum aided and almost supported the slave trade in this country. The poor negroes were bought on the coast of Africa by New England sea captains and paid for with barrels of New England rum. These slaves were then carried on slave ships to the West Indies and sold at a large profit to planters and slave dealers for a cargo of molasses. This was brought to New England, distilled into rum, and sent off to Africa; thus the circle of molasses, slaves, and rum was completed.

In 1708 the West Indies afforded the great demand for negroes; they also furnished the raw material supplying the manufacture of the main merchandise which the thirsty Gold Coast drank up in barter for its poor, banished children. Governor Hopkins stated that for more than thirty years prior to 1764 Rhode Island sent to the Coast annually eighteen vessels carrying 1,800 hogsheads of rum. It displaced French brandies in the trade of the Coast after 1723. The commerce in rum and slaves afforded about £40,000 per annum for remittance from Rhode Island to Great Britain. Molasses and poor sugar, distilled in Boston and more especially in Newport into rum, made the staple export to Africa. Some obtained gallon for gallon of molasses, but the average was 96 to 100. Newport had twenty-two still houses. Boston had the best example, owned by a Mr. Childs. The cost of distilling was five and a half pence per gallon. Cisterns and vats cost fourteen to sixteen shillings per one hundred gallons, in 1735, not including lumber. The quantity of rum distilled was enormous, and in 1750 it was estimated that Massachusetts alone consumed more than 15,000 hogsheads of molasses for this purpose. The average price of molasses in the West Indies was thirteen or fourteen pence per gallon. The consumption of rum in the fisheries and lumbering and ship-building districts was large.

There was no article of merchandise comparable to rum on the African coast. Our forefathers' instincts were neither moral nor immoral; they were simply economic. They had tried dry-goods, and Africa rejected them in favor of the wet. Captain George Scott writes lamenting the purchasing of dry-goods and says, "had we laid out two thousand pounds in rum, bread and flour, it would purchase more in value than all our dry-goods."

The cargo of the Caesar, out-bound, was: eighty-two barrels, six hogsheads and six tierces of New England rum; thirty-three barrels of best Jamaica spirits; thirty-three barrels of Barbadoes rum; twenty-five pairs of pistols; two casks of musket-balls; one chest of hand arms; twenty-five cutlasses. The return cargo was: in the hold on board the scow Caesar, one hundred and fifty-three adult slaves, and two children.

The ships were light of draught and built for speed. The captain and the crew were men little troubled with scruples touching the work they had to do. Once off the coast of Mozambique or Guinea, the cargo was rapidly made up. If a band of blacks, moved by curiosity, came round the vessel in a skiff, they were sure to be lured on board, ironed, and hurried into the hold. If a boat's crew went on shore, they came back dragging some wretched man between them. For rum the native princes gladly sold prisoners that their subjects made in war. When every available inch of space had been filled, the slaver turned westward and made for some southern port. The coast line had scarcely disappeared from view when the hatches were taken off and the terrors of the voyage began. Every fine day at sunrise the slaves were driven on deck. Such as were noisy had the thumb-screws put on. Such as were hard to manage were chained in pairs by the arms, or the ankles, or the necks. At the first sign of insurrection the leaders were shot down and cast into the sea. Their food was salt pork and beans. Their sole exercise was dancing and capering about the deck. This they were made to do. If any refused the cat-o'-nine-tails or the rope's end was vigorously applied. When the sun set the whole band went below. The transactions of one of these slavers are preserved in the history of New Bedford and make interesting reading for those who would hold up the Puritan as innocent of the transgression which stains the character of the Cavalier.

Dr. The natives of Annamboe.		
1770		
Apr. 22.	To one hhds. of rum	110

May 1.	To one hhds. of rum	130
May 2.	To one hhds. of rum	105
May 7.	To one hhds. of rum	108
Cr. **Per contra.**		
Apr. 22.	By one woman slave	110
May 1.	By one prime woman slave	130
May 2.	By one boy slave 4 ft. 1 in.	105
May 7.	By one boy slave 4 ft. 3 in.	108

The Southern Planter

Liquor and slavery combined produced the Southern planter, whose life has often been described by various writers. When Yeardley assumed control of affairs in Virginia, the Company required that there should be inserted in all formal grants of land a covenant that the patentees should not apply themselves either wholly or principally to the culture of tobacco, but should divide their attentions among a number of commodities carefully specified in each deed. These consisted of Indian corn, wheat, flax, silk-grass, and wine. Parton, in his *Life of Jefferson*, says that the Virginia planter expended the proceeds of his tobacco in vast ugly mansions, heavy furniture, costly apparel, Madeira wines, fine horses, and slaves.

Another writer says:

"The gentleman of fortune rises about nine o'clock. He may perhaps make an excursion to his stables to see his horses, which is seldom more than fifty yards from his house; he returns to breakfast between nine and ten, which is generally tea or coffee, bread and butter and very thin slices of venison, ham, or hung beef. He then lies down on a pallet on the floor in the coolest room in the house in his shirt and trousers only, with a negro at his head and another at his feet to fan him and keep off the flies; between twelve and one he takes a bombo or toddy, a liquor compounded of water, sugar, rum, and nutmeg, which is made weak and kept cool; he dines between two and three, and at every meal, whatever else there may be, a ham and greens or cabbage is always a standing dish. At dinner he drinks cider, toddy, punch, port, claret, and Madeira, which is generally excellent here; having drank some few glasses of wine after dinner he returns to his pallet, with his two blacks to fan him, and continues to drink toddy or sangaree all the afternoon. Between nine and ten in the evening he eats a light supper of milk, fruit, etc., and almost invariably retires to bed for the night. This is his general way of living in his family when he has no company. No doubt many differ from it, some in one respect and some in another, but more follow it than do not. Pewter cups and mugs were everywhere to be seen and now and then a drinking horn. There were in the house for the purposes of drinking a variety of receptacles, such as the tumbler, the mug, the cup, the flagon, the tankard, and the beaker. The cups were known by a number of names, such as the lignum vitæ, the syllabub, the sack, and the dram. Many planters in moderate circumstances were in possession of a quantity of silver plate."

MacMasters says of the Southern planter: "Numerous slaves and white servants attended them in every capacity that use or ostentation could suggest. On their tables were to be found the luxuries of the Old World and the New, and chief among these stood Madeira and rum. That the men of that generation drank more deeply than the men of this is not to be doubted." Another writer says: "The Maryland gentry ordered champagne from Europe by the cask and Madeira by the pipe and dressed in the latest fashion."

Betting and gambling were with drunkenness and a passion for duelling and running in debt the chief sins of the South Carolina gentleman.

The Indian Tribes

When Gladwyn wrote to Amherst, "If your Excellency still intends to punish the Indians farther for their barbarities it may easily be done without any expense to the crown by permitting a free sale of rum which will destroy them more effectually than fire and sword," he indicated the policy toward the Indian tribes which has been steadily pursued by all civilized nations on the American continent except the French. Irving, in his *Knickerbocker's History of New York*, has stated the truth on this, as he often does on other matters: "Our benevolent forefathers endeavored as much as possible to ameliorate their situation by giving them gin, wine and glass beads in exchange for their peltries, for it seemed the kind-hearted Dutchmen had conceived a great friendship for their savage neighbors; on account of their being pleasant men to trade with, and little skilled in the art of making a bargain." There is extant a letter of Ebenezer Hazard to Silas Deane of date February 25, 1775, in which Hazard says: "I am told the Committee appointed by the House to state the grievances of this Colony, though mostly Tories, have included all those complained of by Congress and mentioned some new ones, particularly the destruction of the Indian Trade by the Quebec Duty Act. You know that trade cannot be carried on without rum. By the Quebec Duty Act no rum may be sold in the Province but what is entered and the duty paid at Quebec or on Lake Champlain. The Virginians, etc., cannot afford to carry their rum to these places to be entered, and consequently can have no trade. This I am very credibly informed is one of the grievances they have enumerated."

There were but few storekeepers in Virginia in early days who were not engaged in the Indian trade. Guns, ammunition, rum, blankets, knives, and hatchets were the articles in greatest demand among the tribes. When in the ordinary course of events a young American in Virginia or elsewhere felt himself impelled to leave the paternal roof he put aside his gun and fishing rod, and asked of his father some money, a slave, and a canoe. His brow grew thoughtful, and he adopted a pipe. With his money he purchased beads, trinkets, blankets, guns, powder, not forgetting for various reasons a supply of rum. With these he purposed laying the foundation of his fortunes as an Indian trader. If the trader had several servants with him or was associated with other traders he would fix his quarters in some large Indian town and send his subordinates to the surrounding villages, with a suitable supply of blankets, guns, hatchets, liquor, tobacco, etc. This wild traffic was liable to every species of disorder, a fruitful source of broils, robberies, and murders. The fur traders were a class of men held in contempt among the Iroquois and known among them by the significant title of Rum Carriers. The white trappers seem to have been as dissipated as the Indians. One writer declares that most of the Canadians drink so much brandy in the morning that they are unfit for work all day. Another says that when a canoe man is tired he will lift a keg of brandy to his lips and drink the raw liquor from the bung-hole, after which, having spoiled his appetite, he goes to bed supperless, so with drink and hardship he is an old man at forty. The type of French trapper left in the old Northwest may still be seen far north in the great fur land; he is idle, devoted to singing, dancing, gossip, and drinking to intoxication; having vanity as his besetting sin. The Jesuits denounced the traffic. Their case was a strong one, but so was the case of their opponents. There was a real and imminent danger that the thirsty savages, if refused brandy by the French, would seek it from the Dutch and English of New York. It was the most potent lure and the most killing bait. Wherever it was found, there the Indians and their beaver skins were sure to go, and the interests of the fur trade, vital to the colony, were bound to go with it. Cadillac was especially incensed against the Jesuits on account of their opposition to the sale of spirits. So strong was their hostility that Louis XIV, in 1694, referred to the Sorbonne for decision the question of allowing French brandy to be shipped to Michilimackinac. The decision of the Council gave to the Northwest its first prohibitory law; and the commandant was not more willing to enforce the order than his successors have been to carry out similar laws. "A drink of brandy after the repast," he maintained, "seems necessary to cook the bilious meats and the crudities which they leave in the stomach." Again, at Detroit, Cadillac quotes from a sermon by Father Carhail, whose wing he was engaged in plucking. The Jesuit had maintained that there was "no power, either human or divine, which can permit the sale of this drink." Hence, you perceive, argues the crafty commandant, "that this Father passes boldly on all matters of state, and will not even submit to the decision of the pope." The question was indeed a hard one for Cadillac. He understood clearly that unless he had liquor to sell to the savages he might as well abandon his post; for the Indians would go straight to the English at Albany where goods were cheap and rum was unlimited. To give up Detroit never entered Cadillac's plan. He therefore chose the middle course. Instead of prohibition he would have high license. In the restrictions which he threw about the traffic in liquors he was both honest and earnest; and, as events proved, he was far in advance of his times. In the report of M. d'Aigrement, who inspected Detroit in 1708, it is mentioned as one of the grievances of the savages against Cadillac that "in order to prevent disturbances which would arise from the excessive use of brandy, he caused it all to be put into the store-house and sold it at the rate of twenty francs a quart. Those who will have brandy, French as well as Indians, are obliged to go to the store-house to drink, and each can obtain at one time only the twenty-fourth part of a quart. It is certain that the savages cannot become intoxicated on that quantity. The price is high, and as they cannot get brandy only each in his turn, it sometimes happens that the savages are obliged to return home without a taste of this beverage, and they seem ready to kill themselves with disappointment. Though the Jesuits refused absolution to all who sold brandy to the Indians, they sold it themselves. LaSalle had detected them in it." Count Frontenac declares that "The Jesuits greatly exaggerate the disorders caused by brandy and they easily convince persons who do not know the interested motives which have led them to harp continually on this string for more than forty years.... They have long wished to have the fur trade entirely to themselves." Appeal was made to the King, who with his Jesuit confessor, guardian of his conscience, on the one side, and Colbert, guardian of his worldly interests, on the other, stood in some perplexity. The case was referred to the fathers of the Sorbonne and they pronounced the selling of brandy to the Indians a mortal sin. It was next referred to the chief merchants and inhabitants of Canada. Each was directed to write his views. The great majority were for unrestricted trade in brandy, a few for limited and guarded trade, and two or three declared for prohibition. Decrees of prohibition were passed from time to time, but they were unavailing. The King was never at heart a prohibitionist. His Canadian revenue was drawn from the fur trade, and the singular argument of the partisans of brandy, that its attractions were needed to keep the Indians from contact with heresy, served admirably to salve his conscience. The Dutch and English being the heretics, he distrusted the Bishop of Quebec, the great champion of the anti-liquor movement. He wrote to Saint Vallier, Laval's successor in the bishopric, that the brandy trade was very useful to the kingdom of France, that it should be regulated, not prevented, that consciences must not be disturbed by denunciations of it as a sin, that the zeal of the ecclesiastics might be affected by personal interests and passions.

From the time, in 1620, when Samoset and Tisquantum brought Massasoit to Plymouth to drink strong waters with the Puritans, liquor played a steady part in all negotiations between the white men and the red men. When Hamor went to visit Powhattan he was received with royal courtesy, "bread was brought in in two great wooden bowls, the quantity of a bushel of sod bread, made up round, of the bygnesse of a tenise-ball, whereof we ate some few." After this repast Hamor and his comrades were regaled with "a great glasse of sacke" and then ushered into the wigwam for the night. From this time on at all Indian negotiations a large percentage of the Indians expected rum or whiskey to be produced.

No other cause has been as prolific of Indian wars as the liquor traffic.

The war of the Indians with the Dutch in 1675 in New York was caused by the sale of liquor and firearms to the Indians, as well as all the trouble that the Dutch ever seem to have had with their Indian neighbors.

Liquor entered largely as a consideration into the purchase of land from the Indians, and the dispute over title and inadequate amounts frequently caused trouble.

In 1675 Robert Livingston purchased a tract of land on the east side of Hudson river, near Catskill, which was paid for in guilders, blankets, shirts, cloth, tin kettles, powder, guns, twenty little looking-glasses, fish hooks, awls, nails, tobacco, knives, strong beer, four stroud coats, two duffel coats, four tin kettles, rum and pipes, ten pairs large stockings, ten pairs small stockings, adzes, paint, bottles, and scissors. The treaty with the Creek Indians was signed on October 21, 1733, when the governor distributed the following presents among the Indians: A laced coat and a laced hat and shirt to each of the chiefs; to each of the warriors, a gun and a mantle of duffils (a coarse woolen cloth with nap and fringe), and to all their attendants coarse cloth for clothing; a barrel of gunpowder; four kegs of bullets; a piece of broadcloth; a piece of Irish linen; a cask of tobacco pipes; eight belts and cutlasses with gilt handles; tape, and of all colors; eight kegs of rum to be carried home to their towns; one pound of powder, one pound of bullets, and as much provision for each one as they pleased to take for their journey home.

In the spring of 1795 the directors of the Connecticut Land Company sent out surveyors through the Mohawk, over the portage of Wood creek, Oneida lake, and the Oswego river to Lake Ontario. At Buffalo the agent bought of the Indians their remaining claim to the lands east of the Cuyahoga river for five hundred pounds, New York currency, two beef cattle, and one hundred gallons of whiskey.

The murder in 1774 without provocation of the family of Logan, a friendly chief of the Cayuga nation and of great influence, Jefferson shows was due to the drunkenness of two traders, Greathouse and Tomlinson, and caused Logan to deliver the speech which is often given in school readers. The Seminole War had the combined causes of slavery and liquor. President Jackson gave slave traders permission to buy slaves of the Seminole Indians. The trader, knowing that the Indians were intoxicated, would induce them to give bills of sale for negroes they did not own, and the complications thus caused led to the Seminole War.

The Black Hawk War was directly caused by the liquor traffic, while the career of Pontiac, the ablest Indian statesman his race ever produced, illustrates that drunkenness was the bane of the Indian race. In the same speech in which Pontiac said, "our people love liquor and if we dwelt near your old village of Detroit, our warriors would be always drunk," he concluded his harangue with the desire that the rum barrel might be opened and his warriors allowed to quench their thirst. His life was ended by an English trader named Williamson, who bribed a strolling Indian of the Kaskia tribe by a barrel of rum to murder him, and for that reward the savage stole softly behind Pontiac while he was meditating in the forest and buried his hatchet in his brain.

Of the influence of the white man on the Indians the less said the better. They eradicated none of his vices and they lent him many of their own. They found him abstinent, and they made him a guzzler of fire water. They found him hospitable, and they made him suspicious and vindictive. They found him in freedom, the owner of a great country: they robbed him of the one, and crowded him out of the other. The Dutch were too much beer drinkers, became with speed rum consumers, and opposed prohibiting the sale of rum to the Indians. William Penn wrote in 1683: "Ye Dutch, Sweed and English have by brandy and specially rum almost debauched ye Indians all." On arriving at a trading post an Indian hunting party would trade perhaps a third of their peltries for fine clothes, ammunition, paint, tobacco, and like articles. Then a keg of brandy would be purchased and the council held to decide who was to get drunk and who was to stay sober. All arms and clubs were taken away and hidden and the orgie would begin, all the Indians in the neighborhood being called in. It was the task of those who kept sober to prevent the drunken ones from killing one another, a task always hazardous and frequently unsuccessful, sometimes as many as five being killed in one night. When the keg was empty brandy was brought by the kettle full and ladled out with large wooden spoons, and this was kept up until the last skin was disposed of. Then, dejected, wounded, lamed, with their fine new shirts torn, their blankets burned, and nothing but the ammunition and tobacco saved, they would start off down the river to hunt, and begin again the same round of alternating toil and drudgery. Nevertheless, with all their rage for brandy they sometimes showed a self control quite admirable in its way. When at a fair, a council, or a friendly visit their entertainers regaled them with rations of the coveted liquor, so prudently measured out that they could not be the worse for it, they would unite their several portions in a common stock, which they would then divide among a few of their number, thus enabling them to attain that complete intoxication which, in their view, was the true end of all drinking. The objects of this benevolence were expected to requite it on a similar future occasion. In 1708, of the sixty-three settlers at Detroit, thirty-four were traders, and the only profitable articles of trade were ammunition and brandy, the English being able to undersell the French in all other commodities. At the time of the sales of furs every house in Montreal was a drinking shop. In a letter of Governor Halderman to Captain Lernoult, dated July 23, 1729, Halderman says: "I observe with great concern the astonishing consumption of rum at Detroit, amounting to seventeen thousand five hundred and twenty gallons a year."

In his notes on Virginia, Jefferson states that the census of 1669 showed that the Indians of Virginia in sixty-two years decreased about one-third, which decrease Jefferson attributes to spirituous liquors and the smallpox. When president, Jefferson recommended that the sale among the Indian tribes of intoxicating liquors be prohibited.

Of the traffic and its effect on the Indians a large amount of practically unanimous evidence can be produced. LeClercq observes with truth and candor that an Indian would be baptized ten times a day for a pint of brandy or a pound of tobacco. Father Etienne Carheil says: "Our missions are reduced to such an extremity that we can no longer maintain them against the infinity of disorder, brutality, violence, injustice, impiety, impurity, insolence, scorn, and insult which the deplorable and infamous traffic in brandy has spread universally among the Indians of these parts. In the despair in which we are plunged, nothing remains for us but to abandon them to the brandy sellers as a domain of drunkenness and debauchery."

On one occasion the French Denonville lectured Dongon, the English governor, for allowing West India rum to be sent to the Long House. "Think you that religion will make any progress while your traders supply the savages in abundance with the liquor, which as you ought to know converts them into demons, and their wigwams into counterparts of hell." One seems to see the Irishman's tongue curl under his cheek as he replies: "Methinks our rum does as little hurt as your brandy, and in the opinion of Christians is much more wholesome."

Politics and Elections

The presidential campaign of 1840 surpassed in excitement and intensity of feeling all which had preceded it. Delegations to the whig conventions carried banners and often had a small log cabin mounted on wheels in which was a barrel of hard cider, the beverage of the campaign. Early in Harrison's campaign comments were made on the elegant style of living in the White House during Van Buren's administration. Van Buren was charged with being an aristocrat and a monarchist while the masses toiled and suffered to pay for his luxurious living. A Richmond newspaper observed derisively of Harrison, "Give him a barrel of hard cider and a pension of two thousand dollars and our word for it he will sit for the remainder of his days contented in a log cabin." Log cabins and hard cider thus became the symbols of a popular crusade. The log cabins were decked in frontier style with coonskins, bunches of corn, strings of peppers and dried apples and the like, and were set up in cities and villages. Inside these cabins copious supplies of cider were on tap to be drunk with gourds. The appropriateness of the symbol came from the fact that Harrison had formerly resided in a western log cabin, and the cider was meant to typify western hospitality. The result was that young and old drank the cider freely and the whig meetings often degenerated into mere drunken carousals, the example of which was especially injurious to the rising generation.

There are men still alive who claim that a single glass of wine drunk by Herschel V. Johnson was responsible for the wreck of the democratic party in 1860 by unfitting him to reply to the speech of Howell Cobb in favor of separate democratic nominations at the Georgia democratic state convention. The Count de Paris says of the vigilance committees that terrorized the South into secession: "The bar-room was generally the place of their meetings. Around the counter on which gin and whiskey circulated freely a few frantic individuals pronounced judgment upon their fellow citizens, whether present or absent."

In one of the Lincoln-Douglas joint debates Douglas described his own father as an excellent cooper. Lincoln said he did not doubt the truth of the statement for he knew of one very good whisky cask he had made. As Douglas was short and thick-set and a heavy drinker the joke was enjoyed.

On another occasion, Douglas said that when he first knew Lincoln, Lincoln was a good bar-tender. Lincoln in admitting that he had sold whisky said Douglas was one of his best customers, adding that he had left his side of the counter but Douglas had stuck to the other side.

Early Defiance of Law

In the last decade of the eighteenth century the Whiskey Rebellion arose from the refusal of the Scotch-Irish whiskey distillers of Pennsylvania to pay the excise on whiskey. If a collector came among them he was attacked, his books and papers taken, his commission torn up, and a solemn promise exacted that he would publish his resignation in the Pittsburgh *Gazette*. If a farmer gave information as to where the stills could be found, his barns were burned. If a distiller entered his stills as the law required, he was sure to be visited by a masked mob. Sometimes his grist-mill was made useless, sometimes his stills destroyed, or a piece of his saw-mill carried away, and a command laid upon him to publish what had been done to him in the *Gazette*. One unhappy man, who had rented his house to a collector, was visited at the dead of night by a mob of blackened and disguised men. He was seized, carried to the woods, shorn of his hair, tarred, feathered, and bound to a tree. They next formed associations of those who, in the language of the district, were ready to "forbear" entering their stills. They ended by working themselves into a fury and calling a meeting of distillers for the 27th of July, at Restone, Old Fort, a town on which the inhabitants have since bestowed the humbler name of Brownsville. From this gathering went out a call for two conventions. One was to meet on the 23d of August at Washington, in Pennsylvania. The date chosen for the meeting of the second was September 7th, and the place Pittsburgh. Both were held. That at Washington denounced the law and called on all good people to treat every man taking office under it with contempt, and withhold from him all comfort, aid, and support. That at Pittsburgh complained bitterly of the salaries of the federal officers, of the rate of interest on the national debt, of the Funding System, of the Bank, and of the tax on whiskey. Meantime the collector for the counties of Washington and Alleghany was set upon. On the day before the Pittsburgh meeting a party of armed men waylaid him at a lonely spot on Pigeon creek, stripped, tarred, and feathered him, cut off his hair, and took away his horse. They were disguised, but he recognized three of the band, and swore out warrants against them in the district court at Philadelphia. These were sent to the marshal; but the marshal was a prudent man, and gave them to his deputy, who, early in October, went down into Alleghany to serve them. He hid his errand, and as he rode along, beheld such signs of the angry mood of the people, and heard such threats, that he came back with the writs in his pocket unserved. And now he determined to send them under cover of private letters, and selected for the bearer a poor, half-witted cow-driver. The messenger knew not what he bore; but when the people found out that he was delivering writs, he was seized, robbed of his horse and money, whipped till he could scarcely stand, tarred, feathered, blindfolded, and tied to a tree in the woods.

In 1794 a process went out from the district court at Philadelphia against seventy-five distillers who had disobeyed the law. Fifty were in the five counties of Fayette, Bedford, Alleghany, Washington, and Westmoreland. Each writ was dated the 13th of May, and each was entered in the docket as issued on the 31st. But the officials were so tardy that it was July when the marshal rode west to serve them. He arrived in the hurry of harvest, when liquor circulated most freely and drunkenness was most prevalent. Yet he served his writs without harm till but one was left. It was drawn against a distiller named Miller, whose house was fourteen miles from Pittsburgh, on the road to Washington. On the morning of July 15th the marshal set out from Pittsburgh to serve it. He found Miller in a harvest field surrounded by a body of reapers. All went well till he was about to return, when one of them gave the alarm. While some threw down their scythes and followed him, others ran back to the house of the brigade inspector near by. There the Mingo creek regiment had gathered to make a select corps of militia as its quota of the eighty thousand minute men required by Congress. All had drunk deeply, and as the messengers came up shouting "The federal sheriff is taking away men to Philadelphia," they flew to arms. Though it was then night many set off at once, and gathering strength as they went, drew up the next morning, thirty-seven strong, before the house of Revenue Inspector Neville, near Pittsburgh. At the head of them was John Holcroft who whitened half the trees in the four counties with the effusions of Tom the Tinker. The inspector demanded what they wished. They answered evasively. He fired upon them. They returned the shot, and were instantly opened on by a band of negroes posted in a neighboring house. At this the mob scattered, leaving six wounded and one dead. Tom the Tinker was a nom-de-guerre which originated from the house of an obnoxious official being pulled to pieces by a mob whose members gave out that they were "mending it." Mending and tinkering being interchangeable terms, the members dubbed themselves "tinkers," and "Tom the Tinker was shortly evolved as the popular watchword of the first rebellion against the United States government."

CHAPTER VIII
Christenings—Marriages—Funerals

In early American history the use of liquor by an infant seems to have been nearly coincident with its entrance into life. A family receipt called *Caudle* has been handed down through the family of Mrs. Johannes de Peyster, and calls for "three gallons of water, seven pounds of sugar, oatmeal by the pound, spice, raisins and lemons by the quart and two gallons of the very best Madeira wine." This was especially served at the baptism of a child, and partaken of extensively by the women. In early times the Puritan women drank cider and Madeira mixed with water, and much scandal was given by the readiness with which the merry wives of Philadelphia joined in their husbands' comfortable potations. The eighteenth century was the drinking era, and our colony followed in no halting measure the jovial fashions of the day. In 1733 the Pennsylvania *Gazette* laments that Philadelphia women, "otherwise discreet," instead of contenting themselves with one good draught of beer in the morning take "two or three drams by which their appetite for wholesome food is destroyed." Women kept ordinaries and taverns from early days. Widows abounded, for the life of the male colonist was hard, exposure was great, and many died in middle age. War also had many victims. Tavern-keeping was the resort of widows of small means then. Many licenses were granted to them to keep victualling houses, to draw wine, and make and sell beer. In 1684 the wife of one Nicholas Howard was licensed "to entertain lodgers in the absence of her husband"; while other women were permitted to sell food and drink but could not entertain lodgers because their husbands were absent from home, thus drawing nice distinctions. A Salem dame in 1645 could keep an ordinary if she provided "a godly man" to manage her business.

Wedding festivities seemed to have caused about the same amount of liquor drinking throughout the country. In the new land weddings and births were joyful events. The colonists broke with the home traditions and insisted on being married at home rather than at church. As civilization advanced and habits grew more luxurious the marriage festivities grew more elaborate and became affairs of serious expense. Scharf, in his *Chronicles of Baltimore*, says the house would be filled with company to dine; the same company would stay to supper. For two days punch was dealt out in profusion. The gentlemen saw the groom on the first floor, and then ascended to the second floor where they saw the bride; there every gentleman, even to one hundred a day, kissed her. Weddings in old Philadelphia were very expensive and harassing to the wedded. The bride's home was filled with company to dine, the same guests usually stayed to tea, while for two days punch was served in great profusion. Kissing the bride and drinking punch seem to have been the leading features of these entertainments.

A custom prevailed in southern Pennsylvania of barring the progress of the coach of the newly married pair by ropes and other obstacles, which were not removed until the groom paid toll in the form of a bottle of wine, or of drinks to his persecutors.

The famous Schuyler wedding cake had, among other ingredients, twelve dozen eggs, forty-eight pounds of raisins, twenty-four pounds of currants, four quarts of brandy, a quart of rum. This was mixed in a wash tub.

From the earliest period funerals seem to have caused more expense and drunkenness than weddings. In Sewell's *Diary* of the date of August 2, 1725, he says of the funeral of Mrs. Catherine Winthrop: "Had good birth-cake, good wine, Burgundy and Canary, good Beer, oranges and pears." The Puritan funerals were accompanied with so much drinking that a law had to be passed to check the extravagance. In Massachusetts one funeral cost six hundred pounds. Parker, in his history of Londonderry, says:

"Their funeral observances were of a character in some respects peculiar. When death entered their community and one of their members was removed, there was at once a cessation of all labor in the neighborhood. The people gathered together at the house of mourning, observed a custom which they had brought with them from Ireland, called a 'wake' or watching with the dead, from night to night until the interment. These night scenes often exhibited a mixture of seriousness and of humor which appear incompatible. The Scriptures would be read, prayer offered, and words of counsel and consolation administered; but ere long, according to established usage, the glass with its exhilarating beverage, must circulate freely. Although funeral sermons were seldom if ever delivered on the occasion, yet there would be usually as large a congregation as assembled on the Sabbath. Previous to the prayer, spirit was handed round, not only to the mourners and bearers, but to the whole assembly. Again after prayer, and before the coffin was removed, the same was done. Nearly all would follow the body to the grave, and at their return the comforting draught was again administered, and ample entertainment provided. Many a family became embarrassed in consequence of the heavy expenses incurred, not so much by the sickness which preceded the death of one of its members, as by the funeral services as then observed, and which, as they supposed, respect for the dead required."

In New York state before a burial took place a number of persons, usually friends of the dead, watched the body throughout the night, liberally supplied with various bodily comforts, such as abundant strong drink, plentiful tobacco and pipes, and newly-made cakes. These watchers were not wholly gloomy nor did the midnight hours lag unsolaced. A Dutch funeral was costly, the expenditure for gloves, scarfs, and rings was augmented in New York by the gift of a bottle of wine and a linen scarf. At the funeral of Louis Wingard, in Albany, the attendance was large, and many friends returned to the house and made a night of it. These sober Albany citizens drank a pipe of wine, and smoked much tobacco. They broke hundreds of pipes and all the decanters in the house, and wound up by burning all their funeral scarfs in a heap in the fireplace. At Albany the expense reached the climax. The obsequies of the first wife of Stephen Van Renssalaer cost $20,000; two thousand linen scarfs were given and all the tenants were entertained several days.

On Long Island a young man of good family began his youth by laying aside money in gold coin for his funeral, and a superior stock of wine was also stored for the same occasion. In Albany a cask of choice Madeira was bought for the wedding and used in part; the remainder was saved for the funeral of the bridegroom. Up the Hudson were the vast manors of the Beekmans, Livingstons, Van Renssalaers, Schuylers, and Johnsons, where these patroons lived among and ruled over their tenantry like the feudal lords of old England. When a member of the Van Renssalaer family died, the tenants, sometimes amounting to several thousand, says Bishop Kip, came down to Albany to pay their respects to his memory, and to drink to the peace of his soul in good ale from his generous cellars. At the burial of Philip Livingston, in New York, services were performed at both his house and at the manor house. The funeral is thus described in a journal of the day: "In the City the lower rooms of most of the houses in Broadstreet, where he resided, were thrown open to receive visitors. A pipe of wine was spiced for the occasion, and to each of the eight bearers, with a pair of gloves, mourning ring, scarf and handkerchief, a monkey spoon was given. At the manor these ceremonies were all repeated, another pipe of wine was spiced, and besides the same presents to the bearers, a pair of black gloves and a handkerchief were given to each of the tenants. The whole expense was said to be five hundred pounds." At funerals in old New York it was customary to serve hot wine in winter and sangaree in summer. Burnt wine was sometimes served in silver tankards. Death among the Dutch involved much besides mourning. "Bring me a Barrel of Cutt Tobacco, some long pipes, I am out also six silver Tankards. Bottles, Glasses, Decanters we have enough. You must bring Cinnamon and Burnt wine, for we have none," writes Will Livingston, in 1756, on the death of his mother.

Here is the funeral bill of Peter Jacobs Marinus, one of the most prominent of old time New York merchants, who died in the latter part of the seventeenth century:

	£	s.	d.
To 29 galls of Wyne at 6s. 9d. per gallon,	9	15	9
To 19 pairs of gloves at 2s. 3d.	2	4	3
For bottles and glass broke, paid		3	7
Paid 2 women each 2 days attendance		15	
Paid a suit of mourning for ye negro woman freed by ye testator, and making	3	4	7
Paid for 800 cookies & 1½ gross of pipes, at 3s. 3d.	6	7	7
Paid for Speys [spice] for ye burnte wyne and sugar,		1	1
Paid to the sexton and bell ringer for making ye grave and ringing ye bell,	2	2	0
Paid for ye coffin,	4		
Paid for gold and making 14 mourning rings,	2	16	

Paid for 3 yards beaver stuff at 7s. 6d. buttons, and making it for a suit of mourning,	1	14	6
Paid for ½ vat of single Beer,		7	6
Whole amount of funeral charges is	31	6	8

It should be noted that one of the perquisites of the doctor's office was the sale of spices, and on the occasion of funerals they did a thriving business.

In 1764 a reform movement swept through the northern colonies and stopped this extravagance at funerals, so that when Judge Clark died in New Jersey, in 1765, there was no drinking at his funeral. Previous to this time it was not unusual for testators to direct that no liquor should be distributed at their funeral, just as today the request is made in regard to funerals that no flowers be sent.

That the funeral of President Lincoln cost the city of Chicago over eight hundred dollars for the "mourners" was revealed lately in an old whisky and wine bill discovered by City Clerk John R. McCabe. The bill is headed:

Report of Comptroller of amount paid for wine and whisky furnished members of the legislature and the "mourners" at the obsequies of the late president, accepted and filed August 7, 1865.

48 bottles of wine	$216.00
12 bottles whisky	30.00
Wine for Congressional Committee	199.00
Wine & Whisky extras, Supervisors room,	24.00
	$469.00

CHAPTER IX
Vendues—Chopping Bees—House Bees—Wood Spells—Clearing Bees

In a new settlement more than half the houses were log cabins. When a stranger came to such a place to stay, the men built him a cabin and made the building an occasion for sport. The trees felled, four corner men were elected to notch the logs, and while they were busy the others ran races, wrestled, played leap-frog, kicked the hat, fought, gouged, gambled, drank, did everything then considered amusement. It was not luck that made these raisings a success. It was skill and strength, and powers of endurance, which could overcome and surmount even the quantity of vile New England rum with which the workmen were plied during the day. In the older and more settled parts of the country when the first stones of a new wall were laid the masons were given a case of brandy, an anker of brandy, and thirty-two gallons of other liquid. When the beams were carried in by eight men they had a half-barrel of beer for every beam; when the beams were laid two barrels of strong beer, three cases of brandy, and seventy-two florins' worth of small beer. This was the case in 1656 when the old fort at Albany was removed and a new one built. A tun of beer was furnished to the pullers down, and in addition to the above items the wood carriers, teamsters, carpenters, stone cutters, and masons had, besides these special treats, a daily dram of a gill of brandy apiece, and three pints of beer at dinner. They were dissatisfied and solicited another pint of beer. Even the carters who brought wood and boatmen who floated down spars were served with liquor. When the carpenters placed the roof tree a half-barrel of liquor was given them; another half-barrel of beer under the name of tiles beer went to the tile setters. The special completion of the winding staircase demanded five guilders' worth of liquor. When the house was finished a *Kreag* or house warming of both food and drink to all the workmen and their wives was demanded and refused. Well might it be refused, when the liquor bill without it amounted to seven hundred and sixteen guilders. The whole cost of the fort was twelve thousand, two hundred and thirteen guilders, or about three thousand, five hundred dollars. The liquor bill was about three hundred dollars. When the building was completed it was christened by breaking over it a bottle of rum.

Chopping bees were the universal method among pioneers of clearing ground in newly settled districts. Sometimes this bee was held to clear land for a newly married couple, or a new neighbor, or one who had had bad luck; but it was just as freely given to a prosperous farmer though plentiful thanks and plentiful rum were the only reward of the willing workers.

Lyman Beecher, in his autobiography, describes the ministers wood spell, which was a bee held for the purpose of drawing and cutting the winter's supply of wood for the clergyman, and a large amount of beer and cider was provided for the consumption of the parishioners.

Old Ames, of Dedham, Massachusetts, in 1767, describes a corn-husking as follows:

"Possibly this leafe may last a Century and fall in the hands of some inquisitive person for whose entertainment I will inform him that now there is a custom amongst us of making an entertainment at husking of Indian corn whereto all the neighboring swains are invited, and after the corn is finished they like the Hottentots give three cheers or huzzars, but cannot carry in the husks without a Rhum bottle; they feign great exertion but do nothing till Rhum enlivens them, when all is done in a trice, then after a hearty meal about ten o'clock at night they go to their pastimes."

In 1687 William Fitzhugh wrote to Nicholas Hayward, then in England, as follows: "Upon finishing the first line at your corner tree on the Potomac your brother Sam, myself and some others drank your health." The diary of old Governor Spottswood confirms the custom of drinking at the completion of a survey, for in 1716 he with some other Virginia gentlemen and their retainers, a company of rangers and four Indians, fifty-four persons in all, journeyed over the Blue Ridge mountains and descended to the Shenandoah Valley. After drinking the King's health they descended the western slope to the river, which they crossed and named "Euphrates." The governor took formal possession of the region for George I., of England. Much light is thrown on the convivial habits of Virginians at that time by an entry found in the diary of the chroniclers: "We got all the men together and loaded their arms, and we drank the King's health in champagne and fired a volley, the prince's health in Burgundy and fired a volley, and all the rest of the royal family in claret and a volley; we drank the Governor's health and fired another volley. We had several sorts of liquor, viz: Virginia red wine and white wine, Irish usquebaugh, brandy, shrub, two sorts of rum, champagne, canary, cherry punch, cider, etc."

It was the custom when land was transferred that a libation should be poured to Bacchus, and to such an extent was this carried that when Peter Jefferson, the father of Thomas Jefferson, purchased four hundred acres of Virginia land from his old friend and neighbor, William Randolph, of Tuckahoe, the consideration jovially named in the deed is given as "Henry Weatherbourne's Biggest Bowl of Arrack Punch."

The breaking of roads furnished another occasion for the consumption of liquor, and is well described by Whittier:

Next morn we wakened with the shout
Of merry voices high and clear;
And saw the teamsters drawing near
To break the drifted highways out.
Down the long hillside treading slow
We saw the half-buried oxen go,
Shaking the snow from heads uptost,
Their straining nostrils white with frost.
Before our door the straggling train
Drew up, an added team to gain.
The elders threshed their hand a-cold,
Passed, with the cider mug, their jokes
From lip to lip.

Traveling and Taverns

Traveling in ye olden time was by stage going at the rate of ten miles an hour, always stopping at taverns for meals and giving passengers an opportunity to visit the bar to imbibe Holland gin and sugar-house molasses, a popular morning beverage. When the Revolution came most of these vehicles ceased to ply between the distant cities; horseback traveling was resumed, and a journey of any length became a matter of grave consideration. On the day of departure the friends of the traveler gathered at the inn, took a solemn leave of him, drank his health in bumpers of punch, and wished him God-speed on his way. It was no uncommon thing for one who went on business or pleasure from Charleston to Boston or New York to consult the almanac before setting out and to make his will. A traveler was a marked man, and his arrival at an ordinary was the signal for the gathering of all who could crowd in to hear his adventures and also the news. Colonel Byrd was a typical cavalier, and in writing of his visit to Germanna shows an appreciation of the good things of life, with a hearty good will toward his neighbor and especially his neighbor's wife, and a zest for all good things to eat and drink. In his trips he smacks his lips over the fat things that fall in his way. Now it is a prime rasher of bacon, fricasseed in rum; now a capacious bowl of bombo. He tells how he commended his family to the Almighty, fortified himself with a beefsteak, and kissed his landlady for good luck, before setting out on his travels.

The liquor traffic added to the discomforts of travel by water. At New York until the rude steamboats of Fulton made their appearance on the ferry, the only means of transportation for man and beast were clumsy row-boats, flat bottomed, square ended scows with sprit-sails, and two masted boats called periaguas. In one of these, if the day were fine, if the tide were slack, if the waterman were sober, and if the boat did not put back several times to take in belated passengers who were seen running down the hill, the crossing might be made with some degree of speed and comfort and a landing effected at the foot of the steps at the pier which, much enlarged, still forms part of the Brooklyn slip of the Fulton Ferry.

Near Philadelphia at Gloucester Point, if the wind and tide failed, the vessel dropped anchor for the night. If passengers were anxious to be landed in haste they were charged half a dollar each to be rowed ashore. At one in the morning the tide again turned. But the master was then drunk and before he could be made to understand what was wanted the tide was again ebbing and the boat aground.

In the west and south the taverns were generally bad. When Silas Deane and his fellow delegates went down to the Continental Congress in 1774 they found "no fruit, bad rum, and nothing of the meat kind but salt pork." At another tavern they had to go out and "knock over three or four chickens to be roasted for their dinner." No porter was to be had at another inn, and the one palatable drink was some bottled cider.

The Marquis de Chastelleux writes of this region in 1790 in his *Travels in North America*. Landing on a dark night at Courtheath's Tavern the landlord complained that he was obliged to live in this out-of-the-way place of Pompton. He expressed surprise at finding on the parlor table copies of Milton, Addison, Richardson, and other authors of note. The cellar was not so well stocked as the library. He could get nothing but vile cider brandy, of which he must make grog. The bill for a night's lodging and food for himself, his servants and horses, was $16.00.

Much might be written about the taverns, which from the very beginning played an important part in this cheerful, prosperous, unplagued colonial life. Their faded signboards swung in every street, and curious old verses still remain to show us what our wise forefathers liked to read. One little pot-house had painted on its board these encouraging lines:

This is the tree that never grew,
This is the bird that never flew;
This is the ship that never sailed,
This is the mug that never failed.

It was not against every tavern that the reproach could be brought that each person could not have a room to himself, or at least clean sheets without paying extra. Many a New England village inn could, in the opinion of the most fastidious Frenchman, well bear comparison with the best to be found in France. The neatness of the rooms, the goodness of the beds, the cleanliness of the sheets, the smallness of the reckoning, filled him with amazement. Nothing like them was to be met with in France. There the wayfarer who stopped at an ordinary overnight slept in a bug-infested bed, covered himself with ill-washed sheets, drank adulterated wine, and to the annoyance of greedy servants was added the fear of being robbed. But in New England he might with perfect safety pass night after night at an inn whose windows were destitute of shutters, and whose doors had neither locks nor keys. Save the post office it was the most frequented house in town. The great room with its low ceiling and neatly sanded floor, its bright pewter dishes and stout-backed, slat-bottomed chairs ranged along the walls, its long table, its huge fireplace, with the benches on each side, where the dogs slept at night, and where the guests sat when the dip candles were lighted, to drink mull and flip, possessed some attractions for every one. The place was at once the town hall and the assembly room, the court house and the show tent, the tavern and the exchange. There the selectmen met. There the judges sometimes held court. On its door were fastened the list of names drawn for the jury, notices of vendues, offers for reward for stray cattle, the names of tavern haunters, the advertisements of the farmers who had the best seed-potatoes and the best seed-corn for sale. It was at the "General Green," or the "United States Arms," or the "Bull's Head" that wandering showmen exhibited their automatons and musical clocks, that dancing masters gave their lessons, that singing school was held, that the caucus met, that the Colonel stopped during general training. The tavern porch was the rallying point of the town; hither all news came; here all news was discussed; hence all news was disseminated. DeWitt Clinton in his famous letters on political parties says: "In every county or village inn the barroom is the coffee room exchange, or place of intelligence, where all the quid nuncs and newsmongers and politicians of the district resort." Many were the good reasons that could be given to explain and justify attendance at an old-time tavern. One was the fact that often the only newspaper that came to town was kept therein. This dingy tavern sheet often saw hard usage, for when it went its rounds some could scarcely read it, some but pretend to read it. One old fellow in Newburyport opened it wide, gazed at it with interest, and cried out to his neighbor in much excitement: "Bad news! Terrible gales, terrible gales, ships all bottom side up," as indeed they were in his way of holding the news sheet. The extent and purposes to which the tavern sheet might be applied can be guessed from the notice written over the mantel-shelf in the taproom: "Gentlemen learning to spell are requested to use last week's news-letter." A picturesque and grotesque element of tavern life was found in those last leaves on the tree, the few of Indian blood who lingered after the tribes were scattered and nearly all were dead. These tawnies could not be made as useful in the tavern yard as the shiftless and shifting negro element that also drifted to the tavern, for the eastern Indian never loved a horse as did the negro, and seldom became handy in the care of horses. These waifs of either race, the half-breeds of both races, circled around the tavern chiefly because a few stray pennies might be earned there, and also because within the tavern were plentiful supplies of cider and rum.

In Pennsylvania the Moravians became famous for their inns. The "Nazareth," the "Rose," and the "Crown" at Bethlehem were well known. The story of the Rose Tavern is prettily told by Professor Reichel, under the title "A Red Rose from The

Olden Time," it being built on land leased by William Penn, on the rent of one red rose. The best one of all however was "The Sun" at Bethlehem, which was familiar for nearly a century to all the people from Massachusetts to the Carolinas. At different times the inn has entertained beneath its roof nearly all the signers of the Declaration of Independence, most of the members of the Continental Congress, and all the presidents of the United States down to Lincoln. That the wines were remarkable and that the inn had its brand of Madeira, goes without saying. The early Moravians lived largely on game, and cultivated a great variety of vegetables. Deer and grouse were very abundant on the barrens in the manor of the Red Rose. It was long a favorite sporting ground for Philadelphians, and the resort of colonial governors. The wayfarers at the inn lived on all delicacies in the greatest abundance, together with the famous fruit, trout, shad, and wild strawberries. Foreigners who stopped there invariably declared that the inn was fully equal to the best in Europe. It was owned and managed by the Moravian church as part of its communal system.

A good southern hotel of which there were few was a large brick building with a long veranda in front. For a shilling and sixpence, Virginia currency, the traveler was shown to a neat bed in a well furnished room up one flight of stairs. On the wall was fastened a printed table of rates. From this he learned that breakfast cost two shillings, and dinner with grog or toddy was three; that a quart of toddy was one and six, that a bottle of porter was two and six, and that the best Madeira wine sold for six shillings a quart. When he rose in the morning he washed his face, not in his room, but on the piazza, and ate his breakfast in the coolest of dining rooms, at a table adorned with pewter spoons and china plates. Off at one side was a tub full of water wherein melons and cucumbers, pitchers of milk and bottles of wine, were placed to cool. Near by was a water case which held the decanters. If he called for water a wench brought it fresh from the spring, and he drank from a glass which had long been cooling in a barrel which stood in one corner of the room. In winter the fire blazed high on the hearth, and the toddy hissed in the noggin; in summer the basket of fruit stood in the breeze-swept hall, and lightly clad black boys tripped in bearing cool tankards of punch and sangaree.

For his lodging and his board, if he ate a cold supper, and was content with one quart of toddy, he paid to the landlord of the Eagle ten shillings, Virginia currency, or one dollar and sixty-six cents federal money, each day. As to New York taverns, in a letter written by Dr. Mitchel in September, 1794, he states: "The Tontine Coffee House, under the care of Mr. Hyde is the best hotel in New York. He sets from twelve to sixteen dishes every day. He charges for a years board without liquor Three Hundred and Fifty to Four Hundred Dollars."

In Gloucester, Massachusetts, as in other towns the selectmen held their meetings in the tavern. There were five selectmen in 1744, whose salary was five dollars apiece. Their tavern bill, however, amounted to thirty pounds. The following year the citizens voted the selectmen a salary of five pounds apiece and "to find themselves."

In 1825 the expense of living at the Indian Queen in Washington was not great. The price of board was $1.75 per day, $10.00 a week, or $35.00 a month. Brandy and whiskey were placed on the tables in decanters to be drunk by the guests without additional charge therefor. A bottle of real old Madeira imported into Alexandria was supplied for $3.00; sherry, brandy, and gin were $1.00 per bottle, and Jamaica rum $1.00. At the bar toddies were made with unadulterated liquor and lump sugar, and the charge was twelve and a half cents a drink.

CHAPTER X
Extent and Effect of the Traffic at Flood Tide

In 1648 one-fourth of the buildings of New Amsterdam, or New York, were tap-houses.

In his notes on Virginia, Jefferson states that in 1682 there were in Virginia fifty-three thousand, two hundred and eighty-nine free males above twenty-one years of age and one hundred and ninety-one taverns. About this time their number was so great that they were limited by law in each county to one at the court house and one at the ferry.

The diary of Judge Sewall shows that in 1714 Boston had a population of ten thousand, with thirty-four ordinaries, of whom twelve were women; four common victuallers, of whom one was a woman; forty-one retailers of liquor, of whom seventeen were women, and a few cider sellers.

As soon as the white settlers had planted themselves at Pittsburgh they made requisition on Philadelphia for six thousand kegs of flour and three thousand kegs of whiskey. There were distilleries on nearly every stream emptying into the Monongahela.

The Chicago directory for 1830 classified its business interests as taverns, two; Indian traders, three; butchers, one; merchants, one; with a poll list of thirty-two voters.

So much seed sown from the earliest times produced a bountiful harvest. In 1633 Winthrop complains that workmen were idle in spite of high wages because they spent so much in tobacco and strong waters. About this time drunkenness greatly increased and deprived the custom of bundling of whatever innocence it may have had remaining.

Josselyn, in 1675, gives a graphic description of the extravagance and drunkenness of the cod fishermen, stating that at the end of each voyage they drank up their earnings. In this year Cotton Mather said every house in Boston was an ale house. In 1696 Nathaniel Saltonstall, of Haverhill, Massachusetts, a judge who had refused to sit in the Salem witchcraft cases, wrote a letter to the Salem court remonstrating against licensing public houses. In 1678 Dr. Increase Mather said: "Many of the rising generation are profane, drunkards, swearers licentious and scoffers at the power of godliness." Dankers and Sluyter, in 1680, comment on the puritanical laws and say, "drinking and fighting occur there not less than elsewhere and as to truth and true godliness you must not expect more of them than of others."

The Reverend John Miller, in his history of New York, says: "'Tis in this country a common thing even for the meanest persons as soon as the bounty of God has furnished them with a bountiful crop to turn what they can as soon as may be into money, and that money into drinks, at the same time when their family at home have nothing but rags to resist the winter's cold; nay if the fruits of their plantations be such as are by their own immediate labor convertible into liquor such as cider, perry, etc., they have scarce the patience to wait till it is fit for drinking but inviting their boon companions they all of them neglecting whatever work they are about, set to it together and give not over till they have drunk it off. And to these sottish engagements they will make nothing to ride ten or fifteen miles and at the conclusion of one debauch another is generally appointed except their stock of liquor fail them." In his history of New Haven Henry Atwater states: "A brew-house was regarded as an essential part of a homestead, and beer was on the table as regularly as bread." When in Stuyvesant's day it was reported that fully one-fourth of the houses in New Amsterdam were devoted to the sale of brandy, tobacco, and beer, Mr. Roberts observed:

"Their existence tells the story of the habits of the people. It was when Governor Sloughter was besotted with drink that he signed the illegal death warrant of Leisler; it was when the informer Kane was possessed by the fumes of liquor of the tavern, that he foisted upon the terrified colonists the lying details of the shameful negro plot; it was when the representative of the most powerful family in the province, Chief Justice DeLancey, and Governor Clinton, the proxy of the King, were 'in their cups' that a personal quarrel led to antagonisms that threatened the welfare of the colony. Indeed the deep hold that this vice had upon the morals of the entire colony seemed to repeat and emphasize the wisdom of the name which the earlier Spanish in an intercourse had fastened upon its leading town—Monafos—'the place of the drunken men.'"

Whiskey as Money

In a large part of the territory now the United States the early settlers lived in the rudest kind of log cabins and knew no other money than whiskey and the skins of wild beasts. In 1780, after the collapse of the continental currency, it seemed there was no money in the country, and in the absence of a circulating medium there was a reversion to the practice of barter, and the revival of business was thus further impeded. Whiskey in North Carolina and tobacco in Virginia did duty as measures of value. In Pennsylvania what a bank bill was at Philadelphia or a shilling piece at Lancaster, whiskey was in the towns and villages that lay along the banks of the Monongahela river. It was the money, the circulating medium of the country. A gallon of good whiskey at every store in Pittsburgh, and at every farmhouse in the four counties of Washington, Westmoreland, Alleghany, and Fayette, was the equivalent of a shilling. And when, in 1797, the government began to coin new money for the people, the new coins did not, many of them, go far from the seaports and great towns. In the country districts, in the Ohio valley, on the northern border they were still unknown. The school-master received his pittance in French crowns and Spanish half-joes. The boatmen were paid their hire in shillings and pence, and if perchance some traveler paid his reckoning at a tavern with a few American coins, they were beheld with wonder by every lounger who came there to smoke and drink.

Temperance Societies

The first prohibitory law was that of Georgia, in 1733, and the first dawn of temperance sentiment was undoubtedly the pledge of Governor Winthrop, still earlier than this, when he announced his famous discountenance of health drinking. This first of all temperance pledges in New England is recorded in his diary in language as temperate as his intent:

"The Governor, upon consideration of the inconveniences which have grown in New England by drinking one to another, restrained it at his own table, and wished others to do the like; so it grew little by little, into disuse."

Lyman Beecher claims the Massachusetts temperance society formed in 1813 to be the first one, the pledge of its members being to discontinue the use of liquor at entertainments, funerals, and auction sales, and to abstain from furnishing laborers with grog during haying time, as was then the custom. John B. Gough, however, mentions the constitution of a temperance society formed in New York in 1809, one of whose by-laws was, "Any member of this association who shall be convicted of intoxication shall be fined a quarter of a dollar, except such act of intoxication shall take place on the Fourth of July, or any other regularly appointed military muster."

In 1817 a committee of New York citizens appointed to investigate the causes of pauperism reported that seven-eighths of the paupers were reduced to abject poverty by the sale of liquor. As far back as 1809 the Humane Society found eighteen hundred licensed dramshops scattered over the city, retailing liquor in small quantities, and offering every inducement to the poor to drink.

New Hampshire required a selectman of each town to post the names of tipplers in every tavern and fined anyone ten dollars who sold them liquor. About this same time the legislature of Pennsylvania passed a law authorizing the governor to appoint a commission of nine to investigate the causes of pauperism in Philadelphia, and to report to the next legislature. The farmers of Upper Providence township, Pennsylvania, met in the school house just before harvest time and agreed not to give liquor to their harvest hands, nor to use it in the hay field or during harvest, nor to allow any one in their employ to use it. A general movement for temperance swept over the Atlantic states. The Portland Society, auxiliary to the Massachusetts Society for Suppressing Intemperance, reported that out of eighty-five persons in the workhouse, seventy-one became paupers through drink. A grand jury at Albany drew a picture of their city quite as dismal, and presented the immense number of dramshops and corner groceries where liquor was retailed by the cent's worth as an evil and a nuisance to society.

One of the most interesting documents in early temperance agitation is the letter of the mayor of Philadelphia in 1821, showing the condition of the liquor traffic at that time. He pointed out the dangers of the tippling houses and corner groceries, where liquor was sold by the cent's worth to children five years old, and paid for often with stolen goods.

The liquor traffic left an indelible impress upon the geography of the country. The oldest American reference to the word RUM is in the Massachusetts statute of 1657 prohibiting the sale of strong liquors "whether known by the name of rum, strong water, brandywine, etc." The Dutch in New York called rum brandywine, and it conferred its name upon the river which in turn gave its name to one of the most famous battles of the Revolution. Among places may be found such names as Rumford, Wineland, Winesburg, and others.

When in 1828 Mr. Garrison assumed the editorial control of the *Journal of the Times* at Bennington, Vermont, he distinctly avowed that he had three objects in view, "The suppression of Intemperance and its associate vices, the gradual emancipation of every slave in the Republic, the perpetuity of the national peace." He contributed to the third object; he accomplished the second; the first problem he left unsolved as a bequest to this generation.